5 KEYS TO BUILDING LIFELONG HEALTHY RELATIONSHIPS

OVERCOMING TRUST CONCERNS, SETTING BOUNDARIES, HANDLING CONFLICT POSITIVELY FOR A STRONG, COMMITTED PARTNERSHIP IN HAPPINESS AND LOVE

ARIANE S. TURPIN

THE LUXE NORTH
—PUBLISHING—

Published by The Luxe North Publishing

Montreal, QC, Canada

www.arianeturpin.com

CONTENTS

FREE GIFT #1 FOR MY READERS

Just for you! As a thank you for being my valued reader, you can get this free ebook on 9 Guided Meditations to Deepen Your Intimacy and Communication in Your Relationship.

Visit ebook.arianeturpin.com/9meditations or scan the above QR code to access it.

INTRODUCTION

Meet Alexis and Jeremy. Alexis and Jeremy were a profoundly in love couple who had been together for a number of years. They felt deeply committed to one another, had a strong connection, and shared many common ideals.

But as time passed, Alexis and Jeremy's relationship started to face some difficulties. They discovered that they were fighting more often and having trouble communicating clearly. They were having trouble establishing and upholding limits with one another since their mutual trust was deteriorating. They felt worn out and detached because even the tiniest disagreements appeared to turn into enormous clashes.

Alexis and Jeremy came to the conclusion that in order to save their marriage, they needed to seek help. They started the difficult but gratifying task of mending their relationship after finding a therapist who specialized in working with couples.

Through their sessions, Alexis and Jeremy discovered the five essential elements of a good relationship: respect for one another's boundaries, effective communication, mutual trust, handling conflict constructively, and relational self-care. They understood the importance of these elements in creating a solid and long-lasting alliance.

Alexis and Jeremy started to notice a significant improvement in their relationship as they worked through their problems under the direction of their therapist. They learned to communicate more clearly and to listen more deeply to one another. They began to establish and respect one another's boundaries, which made them feel more secure and protected in their union. Instead of focusing on winning fights, they started to handle conflict in a more constructive manner.

Perhaps most importantly, Alexis and Jeremy began to prioritize their own self-care and the health of their relationship. They scheduled frequent date nights, long walks, and other enjoyable activities into their schedules. They developed the ability to express their needs and help one another in reaching both their personal and shared goals.

Alexis and Jeremy's union developed over time into a contented, loving, and successful one. With each passing day, their love for one another grew stronger, and they felt closer than ever.

The story of Alexis and Jeremy serves as a potent reminder of the value of prioritizing our relationships and the five essential elements of a healthy relationship. The principles of mutual trust, effective communication, setting and respecting boundaries, handling conflict constructively, and relational self-care can help you lay the groundwork for a happy, loving, and fulfilling relationship, regardless of whether you're just beginning a new one or hoping to strengthen an existing one.

The human experience is not complete without relationships. Relationships have a huge impact on our lives, whether we're talking about romantic relationships, friendships, or ties to our families. They have the power to provide us with great happiness, solace, and contentment, but they can also give us considerable pain, annoyance, and heartache.

We are wired for connection as humans. We yearn for closeness, love, and understanding. We want people to accept us for who we are, hear, and love us. Building and keeping up strong relationships is not always simple, though. It takes time, effort, and a readiness to be openly honest and vulnerable with people.

This book is meant to help you in creating and uphold successful, healthy relationships with your partner. The five key elements of a healthy relationship will help you develop a loving, supportive, and rewarding relationship with your partner.

A healthy relationship is built on **trust**. It is impossible to develop intimacy, speak clearly, or resolve disputes without trust. When you have trust in someone, you can count on them to treat you with respect and be honest with you. It implies that you can express your weaknesses, anxieties, and insecurities without worrying about criticism or rejection.

Over time, developing trust requires displaying consistent acts and behaviors. Open lines of communication, respect for one another, and a readiness to share vulnerability are necessary for building trust. In a relationship, when trust is present, partners feel safe and secure and are better equipped to help one another through the difficulties of life.

A relationship that succeeds depends on **effective communication**. It is the manner in which we communicate to our partner our requirements, feelings, and desires. Active listening, empathy, and a desire to understand one another's views are necessary for effective communication.

It entails being able to communicate your ideas and emotions in a direct, considerate, and nonjudgmental manner.

Building closeness, settling problems and strengthening your connection all depend on effective communication. Open and honest communication between partners helps them better understand one another's wants and desires and enables them to work together to build a successful and meaningful relationship.

Healthy relationships must have clear **boundaries**. They help in creating unambiguous standards for proper conduct and guard against unfair treatment or exploitation of others. Understanding your own needs and limitations and communicating them to your partner in a respectful and transparent manner are both necessary components of setting and upholding boundaries.

The boundaries between partners are acknowledged and respected. Together, they strive to establish a setting where both partners can feel free to express their needs and wants. Partners can develop trust, strengthen their bond, and form a full and rewarding relationship by establishing and observing limits.

All relationships will inevitably experience **conflict**. It is hard for two people to always agree on everything. But the way a couple handles disagreements can make or ruin a union. Positive conflict resolution requires respectfully listening to your partner's point of view, expressing your own ideas and emotions, and cooperating to come up with a workable solution.

Partners are aware that conflict is a normal aspect of being human. They cooperate to resolve problems and disagreements in a healthy and helpful way. Partners can increase trust, strengthen their bond, and forge a more full and happy relationship by handling disagreement constructively.

Relational self-care is the act of caring for oneself while in a relationship. It entails putting your personal pleasure and fulfillment first while simultaneously taking care of your relationship with your partner. Relational self-care entails taking the time to acknowledge your own needs and wants, sharing them with your partner, and cooperating to build a pleasant and rewarding relationship.

Partners are aware of the importance of taking care of themselves for the relationship's overall health. They support their partner's needs while simultaneously putting their own needs for self-care first. Partners can develop a stronger feeling of connection and understanding with one another and a relationship that is mutually supportive and enjoyable by engaging in relational self-care.

These five key elements work together to create a strong, enduring relationship. Building and maintaining a solid, devoted, and encouraging relationship requires each element. Without these elements, relationships run the risk of becoming tense, unfulfilling, and even harmful.

Research in the discipline of psychology emphasizes the significance of these five crucial elements. Several studies have confirmed the beneficial effects of healthy relationships on both our physical and mental well-being. Healthy relationships have been associated with lower stress and depression levels, better cardiovascular health, and even longer lifespans.

Our feeling of purpose and meaning in life, as well as the success of our careers, can all be impacted by the quality of our relationships. In other words, our relationships are crucial to our sense of overall fulfillment and happiness.

Each of these elements will be thoroughly examined in

this book, along with useful tools and techniques for improving your relationship with your partner. I'll share some tips which I've personally found helpful on how to establish rapport, communicate clearly, set and uphold limits, resolve disputes amicably, and engage in relational self-care.

Through consulting the most recent psychological research, I'll offer evidence-based guidance on how to create and maintain a healthy, rewarding relationship. I will also share examples from the actual world and anecdotes to demonstrate how these ideas might be put into practice in daily life.

This book will provide you with the information, advice and support which I hope you will find helpful for creating a solid, meaningful relationship, regardless of how long you have been dating or have been together with your partner, or how recently you started a relationship. I cordially invite you to accompany me on this adventure and experience the satisfaction and fulfillment that come from a healthy, thriving, loving relationship.

PART I

CHAPTER 1: WHAT IS A HEALTHY RELATIONSHIP?

*W*ould you say that your relationship is a healthy one? Do you know what qualities to look for in a partner, and how would you know if you found them? Many people are so focused on finding "the one" or that "spark" that they neglect to consider whether the relationship is healthy for them. Before you can truly achieve contentment and happiness in a relationship with another person, you must stand back and figure out how to create a healthy relationship.

As you begin to consider how to build a healthy relationship, don't instantly focus on the other person or what they do for you. Instead, concentrate on the relationship itself and how the two of you interact. What unique qualities does this relationship possess? What drew you two together in the first place? Shut your eyes and visualize the joy you bring to your lover. Imagine being entirely loved and gratified by someone else. What does that feel like? And most importantly, why does it feel like that?

Consider what it is about this potential relationship that

is so exceptional. Can you express it verbally? It might not be immediately clear to you why it feels so wonderful, but it probably possesses the majority, if not all, of the traits of a healthy relationship.

WHAT IS A HEALTHY RELATIONSHIP?

Everybody has heard the expression "relationship requires work," but what does that really mean?

To be honest, it sounds like drudgery. Who wants to work long hours at an office just to return home to their second job? Wouldn't it be more pleasant to see your relationship as a source of solace, enjoyment, and pleasure?

Power dynamics between the two partners are balanced in a healthy partnership. It calls for honesty, respect, and other virtues. To keep it going, both parties must make constant sacrifices.

A healthy relationship is created when partners fully respect each other's independence, decisions, privacy, space, and viewpoints.

HOW HAPPY ARE PEOPLE IN THEIR RELATIONSHIPS?

Even while Americans may be becoming skeptical about politics, the economy, or even the environment, they continue to believe in the one thing that is more erratic than all of these: LOVE.

According to a recent national survey titled "The Happiness Index: Love and Relationships in America," which was commissioned by eHarmony and carried out by Harris Interactive, 64 percent of Americans describe their romantic relationships with a partner or spouse as "very happy," and nearly 50 percent say they are content with their sexual lives.

Relationship happiness and how to maintain healthy ones are topics that eHarmony often discusses. They wanted to test society and learn more about how American couples relate to one another today. The gender and age dynamics in relationships are changing, which dispels long-held stereotypes about both men and millennials, which is perhaps the most shocking discovery.

According to the latest survey, millennials between the ages of 25 and 34 are the happiest in their relationships. While 19% of Americans say they are unhappy in their relationships, they are finding it desirable to commit to one another for the long term: relationships last an average of 18 years overall, and for respondents over the age of 65, they can last up to 36 years.

The survey also revealed the keys to happiness for the 26% of respondents who claimed to be "completely satisfied" in their committed relationships. They were typically the same age as their partner or spouse, took the time to get to know one another before committing to marriage, and shared a variety of hobbies. They continued to make time for one another even after having children. On the other hand, just 6% of respondents said they were "desperately unhappy" in their relationships. These individuals were more likely to have placed companionship before love, lacked intimacy, and were less likely than the general population to be married.

IS YOUR RELATIONSHIP HEALTHY? (QUESTIONS TO ASK YOURSELF)

It's important to keep in mind that perfect relationships do not exist. Every relationship combines both positive and negative traits. Each party's understanding that relationships require effort is what characterizes a positive bond. Everybody must work to keep the connection strong and fix issues.

We often spend a lot of time discussing how to recognize a bad relationship but little time discussing what makes a healthy relationship. Think about the following:

- Do you value one another?
- Do you trust each other?
- Do you support the goals and initiatives of one another?
- Are you able to retain your sense of self?
- Is communication between you two open and honest?
- Do you share your thoughts, feelings, aspirations, and anxieties with others?
- Is your relationship based on equality and fairness?
- Do you harbor and demonstrate affection?
- Does your partner support your growth?
- Do you desire the same kind of connection?
- Do you have similar future goals?
- Can you be genuine around them?
- Is there a purpose to your time together?
- Do you treat one another properly, giving and receiving equally?
- Can you accept them as they are?
- Do they make your life better or worse?

Your relationship is definitely strong if you largely responded "yes" to the above questions. Each person has unique demands. For instance, some people have greater requirements for affection and openness than others. When your relationship is healthy, each party is able to fulfill their needs.

WHAT MAKES A HEALTHY RELATIONSHIP?

It's possible that they are quite uncommon if we don't see them often. Only 10% of American marriages, according to researchers, are very healthy and happy. In multiple studies employing fMRI scans of the brain, researchers Acevedo and Aron observed that one in ten of the senior couples (married an average of 21 years) displayed the same neuro-chemical reactions when given images of their loved ones as people often do in the early stages of a relationship. They referred to these still-in-love couples as "swans."

What can we learn about healthy relationships from these ones so that we can build our own? Even if finding love hasn't always been easy for you.

Thinking about what makes up a healthy relationship is a stellar thing to do whether you are single, dating Mr. or Ms. Right, or involved in a committed relationship that has been unfulfilling for a long time. Let's look at one of these blissful couples I know.

Jane has a mass of extremely curly hair, is a bit over-weight, and looks like an angel. She is giggling and whispering in her husband Steve's ear while she is seated on his lap. Jane's whispered comments are being laughed at by Steve, a tall, lanky salesperson, as he compares her to Lucille Ball. He lands a kiss on her after softly pushing a hair from her forehead. He receives a warm "Thanks!" from Jane. Despite being at a party with 25 other people, the couple seems to be in their own universe.

A young woman approached the pair and asked if they had just gotten married. Even though it is clear that the answer is no, Jane and Steve laugh heartily and respond, "yes." They've been married for twelve years. They remain wildly in love, nevertheless. They have continued affection for each other as well as mutual closeness and humor. And their pleasant exchanges outnumbered their unpleasant ones 5 to 1. Jane and Steve are a strong, contented couple. But don't give up. They are not the only ones.

Every relationship is unique, and there are a variety of reasons why people come together. Sharing a common vision for what you want your relationship to be and where you want it to go is one of the characteristics that make a relationship healthy. And the only way to determine that is to have a lengthy, honest conversation with your partner.

However, the majority of healthy relationships share a few common traits. Understanding these basic concepts can help you maintain a meaningful, rewarding, and exciting relationship regardless of the problems or shared goals you two may be working on.

TRUST

Any successful relationship needs both people to have trust in one another. According to research, your overall attachment style may have an impact on your capacity to trust others. Early relationships in life have an impact on the expectations you have for subsequent relationships.

You are more inclined to trust prospective partners if your previous relationships were safe, secure, and trustworthy. But, if your previous relationships were erratic and unreliable, you could have to deal with trust issues moving ahead.

Trust is also formed by how couples treat one another. You are more likely to form this trust if your partner treats you well, is reliable, and you know they'll be there for you when you need them.

In order to establish trust, both parties must mutually provide information about themselves. Opportunities to put that trust to the test and evaluate it arise over time. The relationship develops into a significant source of comfort and security as trust deepens. It can be a sign that you lack this crucial trust if you feel like you have to keep things from your partner.

Honesty & Transparency

In a healthy relationship, you should feel free to be who you are. Although there are different levels of openness and self-disclosure in every marriage or relationship, you should never feel as though you have to change who you are or conceal any aspects of who you are. Being open and honest with one another promotes trust in addition to making you feel more connected as a couple.

In a newly established relationship, you could be more reserved and cautious about the information you are willing to divulge. Couples communicate more of their thoughts, opinions, beliefs, hobbies, and memories to one another as their relationship becomes more intimate over time.

This does not imply that you must disclose everything to your partner. Every person deserves their own space and privacy. One of the most important factors is whether each couple is at ease discussing their hopes, anxieties, and feelings. Healthy relationships don't necessarily require constant companionship or sharing of daily activities.

Yet, disagreements over how much honesty should exist in a relationship can occasionally lead to issues. Thankfully, a study indicated that people usually talk to their partner about the issue when they are unsatisfied with their partner's level of openness. This is a great illustration of how honestly discussing a problem can improve a relationship.

It's crucial to discover methods to compromise while still upholding your own limits, even when your partner could have requirements that are different from yours. Setting boundaries establish that each individual has their own wants and expectations, rather than being about secrecy.

A partner who has unhealthily high standards for transparency and honesty may want access to your personal social media accounts and demand to know every little thing about your whereabouts and what you're up to.

Mutual Respect

Those who are in close, healthy relationships appreciate one another. They provide support and safety for one another without mocking or disparaging one another.

There are various ways that couples can appreciate one another. They include the following:

- Creating space in your life for your partner
- Showing interest in their interests
- Letting them be themselves.
- Listening to one another
- Not putting off or stonewalling requests from your partner
- Being considerate and forgiving when one of you makes a mistake.
- Expressing love and gratitude for one another
- Encouraging and supporting your partner in their goals and hobbies

AFFECTION

Fondness and affection are qualities that define healthy relationships. Research has shown that the early passion that marks the start of a new relationship tends to decline over time, but this does not mean that the need for affection, solace, and sensitivity disappears.

Passionate love is characterized by powerful emotions, great longing, and a need to maintain physical contact. Typically, this occurs in the early stages of a relationship. This intense love gradually develops into a compassionate love that is characterized by emotions of adoration, intimacy, trust, and commitment.

Yet it's crucial to keep in mind that everyone has varied physical requirements. There is no ideal level of intimacy or affection. Both parties must be happy with the amount of affection they exchange with one another for a relationship to be considered healthy. Genuine love and affection for one another that is shown in a variety of ways are what make a relationship nurturing.

EXCELLENT COMMUNICATION

Communication skills are necessary for all types of relationships, including romantic and friendship ones.

Although it may seem that the finest relationships are ones that are free of conflict, it is more vital to know how to debate and settle disagreements than it is to just avoid disagreements in order to keep the peace.

Conflict can occasionally be a chance to improve your relationship with your partner. When significant issues need to be resolved, research has shown that conflict may be helpful in intimate relationships, allowing partners to make adjustments that are good for the relationship's future.

Those in healthy relationships can avoid personal attacks when conflicts do occur. Instead, they talk about their thoughts and feelings and try to come to a compromise while still being respectful of and sympathetic to their partner.

GIVE-AND-TAKE

Natural reciprocity is a sign of a strong relationship. It's not about keeping score or believing you owe someone something. You sincerely want to help one another when you do things for one another.

Also, it does not imply that a relationship's give and take is always exactly equal. One partner may occasionally require more assistance and support. In other situations, one partner may merely choose to assume a more caregiver-like role. As long as everyone is comfortable with the dynamic and both partners are receiving the support they require, such imbalances are okay.

WARNING SIGNS OF AN UNHEALTHY RELATIONSHIP

In order to improve over time, we must simultaneously educate ourselves about what makes an unhealthy relationship and train ourselves to do better over time.

Like all relationships, bad ones begin the same way. Although they are exciting, passionate, and enjoyable, they eventually veer into unhealthy terrain.

Because we often mistreat and insult the people we love,

it can be challenging to recognize the warning signs of an unhealthy relationship.

Everybody engages in unhealthy behaviors occasionally, but the likelihood that a relationship may devolve into abuse increases as the number of bad behaviors increases.

Your relationship should promote a feeling of connection, contentment, and joy. Your relationship may be having problems if you typically feel more pressured, anxious, or dissatisfied around your partner.

This list is not exhaustive, as there are many different signs of unhealthy relationships. Yet it might help in highlighting some potential problems.

One of you seeks to change or control the other.

We can never force someone else to change. You should feel at ease enough to bring up a specific behavior if you have concerns about it. It's acceptable to share your emotions and ask them to take change into consideration. Yet it's not acceptable to direct them or make an effort to manage their behavior.

The relationship may not have long-term prospects if they do anything that genuinely irritates you and you are unable to accept it.

Your partner disregards your boundaries.

Every aspect of your relationship might have boundaries, from courteous communication to privacy requirements. Setting boundaries and having people push against them or demand that you change them raises severe red flags.

Maybe you've said, "When I get home from work, I need

privacy. I'm glad to see you, but before we get physical, I need to unwind."

But they keep approaching you as soon as you get home, attempting to kiss you and entice you into the bedroom. They apologize and claim that "they just can't help themselves" when you say no.

You might interpret this as a sign of affection and keep reiterating the boundaries in the hopes that they'll finally understand it. But they act in a way that disregards your needs.

There isn't much time spent together.

Those who like each other's company and wish to spend more time together are likely to form relationships. Your time together may occasionally be disrupted by happenings in your life, although these disruptions are typically brief.

If you often spend less time with each other without a clear explanation, such as problems at home or increased workloads at work, your relationship may be in trouble.

Feeling distant from one another or relieved when you are apart are further red flags. You can even make an effort to justify your absence from one another.

The dynamic feels unbalanced.

Healthy relationships usually have a decent amount of balance. Share your finances evenly, or one partner can undertake more household responsibilities to make up for a lower income. Each relationship differs so there is no one standard way to balance it, but the important thing is that you communicate with each other on what would make it feel balanced for both of you.

Relationship equality, however, can also refer to immaterial concepts like love, communication, and relationship expectations. There may occasionally be times of inequality. One of you may experience a brief loss of income, experience difficulty helping out with duties owing to illness, or experience a decrease in affection due to stress or other emotional upheavals.

Yet, this might become a problem if your relationship feels uneven on a frequent basis in any way.

They make disparaging or harmful remarks about you or other people.

When your partner does something that disturbs you, it is perfectly okay to show concern. Nonetheless, partners in a healthy relationship usually take care to communicate their emotions in positive, constructive ways.

Constantly criticizing one another or saying cruel things out of malice is unhealthy, especially when it comes to decisions of one's own, like what to wear, eat, or watch on television. It's often useless to receive criticism that makes you feel ashamed or inferior to yourself.

Be aware of how they speak about other people. Your relationship may appear to be strong, but if your partner engages in hate speech, uses racial slurs, or makes discriminating statements about others, take into account what this behavior says about them personally.

You don't feel heard in the relationship

If they seem uninterested when you raise a concern or express something that has been on your mind, it's possible that this is why you don't feel heard. Sometimes you can find it difficult to express your viewpoint or bring up critical topics because you fear they'll ignore you.

Of course, miscommunications can occur. But, if you do discuss a problem with them and they appear receptive but don't make any changes or appear to have forgotten all you discussed the following day, that is also a red flag.

You're scared to voice your disagreement.

When partners disagree, they should always feel free to express their differences. Your partner may not appreciate you or your views if they reply to your (different) point of view with contempt, dismissal, or other rudeness.

It might be time to get professional assistance if you find yourself censoring everything you say out of fear of their response or if you constantly feel like you're "stepping on eggshells."

Go to a therapist as soon as you can if you worry about being physically or verbally abused. Don't be afraid to ask your friends and family for help as well.

You don't feel content or at ease around your lover.

Major relationship goals for many people include achieving more happiness and life satisfaction. If you often feel unsettled or sad, the relationship may not be fulfilling your requirements.

This might still occur even when both of you are making an attempt to improve the relationship. Feeling imprisoned and unsatisfied doesn't necessarily indicate that you or your partner did anything "wrong" because people evolve through time. You might just have changed into new individuals that don't mesh well with one another.

Discussions or disagreements are pointless.

Healthy dispute resolution usually results in agreements or compromises. You might not resolve everything right away because maintaining a relationship is a continuous process. But after a chat, you usually feel good about it. Usually, some development is visible.

Generally speaking, it's not a good sign if you find yourself constantly returning to the same topics or talking in circles. Perhaps no matter how much you debate something, nothing ever gets better. Maybe they just gave up on you in the end.

* * *

*E*ven if your relationship appears to be in good shape, taking a step back and considering how you and your partner can improve things can be beneficial. Having the ability to identify issues, including your own, that could endanger the long-term success of your relationship shows your relationship is healthy. You can work together to create a more rewarding relationship by openly examining your relationship.

CHAPTER 2: BUILDING TRUST IN RELATIONSHIPS

*I*f you've ever experienced problems with trust in a relationship, you're not the only one. It might be difficult to trust your partner, especially if you've been the victim of infidelity or betrayal in the past. You might not feel confident in your current relationship because your ex cheated. Or perhaps you worry or suspect that your partner is hiding something from you, leading you to become doubtful of their motives. Learning to trust your partner can be a vulnerable process, regardless of your past experiences.

In BestVPN.com's study of more than 1,000 people worldwide in 2019, the majority of respondents (82%) who had never experienced infidelity expressed perfect trust in their current partner. However, trust dropped to 68% among people who had previously uncovered their partner's infidelity, indicating that bad experiences might have a lasting effect on relationships. Surprisingly, a quarter of those who admitted to cheating said they were exposed to social media and technology.

There are various ways to resolve your trust issues and

feel more secure in your relationship, whether you're trying to mend fences after a betrayal or you just want to feel safer and more stable with your partner. Let's talk about the reasons why trust is important, some possible causes of your trust issues, and the advice from experts on how to begin establishing trust in your relationship.

WHAT IS TRUST IN A RELATIONSHIP?

Trust is the assurance you have in someone's unwavering commitment to and love for you. If you trust someone, you can depend on them, and you may confide in them because you feel safe in their presence.

Any relationship will always have a shaky, unstable foundation without it. It is an essential part of every relationship.

The growth of relationships depends on mutual trust. Think about what it could be like to live a life without trust: you want to tell your partner or spouse a secret but are hesitant; or your partner or spouse reads the messages from their friends, and somehow you suspect they are lying and perhaps messaging some other love interest instead; or they tell you they're going out with people from work, but in your mind you're thinking they might be on a date; and the list goes on. Relationships are challenging to keep up with. If you don't trust each other, every minute of your existence turns into a nightmare.

In actuality, a relationship devoid of trust devolves into chaos and disorder.

UNDERSTANDING THE IMPORTANCE OF TRUST IN A RELATIONSHIP

Trust is essential in order for a relationship to be successful and joyful. Below are a few reasons why trust in a relationship is important.

ENCOURAGES OPTIMISM

Relationships need trust because it enables you to be more open and generous. If you trust your partner, you believe in them and know they have your back, and you are more likely to be tolerant of their flaws or annoying behaviors.

REDUCES CONFLICT

You can also handle disagreement when you have trust. When you have trust in your partner, you are more dedicated to finding answers or inclined to put up with challenges because you feel unified in the causes that are most important to you. If you trust your partner, you are more inclined to give them a chance and be forgiving and see the good in them, even if they do something disappointing.

INCREASES PROXIMITY

Building a strong relationship and foundation on trust is essential. Having confidence in your relationship fosters more safety and intimacy. You feel safe knowing your partner has your back and can be counted on for comfort, care, and support when you have mutual trust.

Your nervous system may also unwind, rest, and reset

when you trust your partner. Your relationship can be a place of healing for both sides by building a solid foundation of trust, especially if this hasn't always been the case in previous relationships with family or ex-partners.

WHAT MIGHT HAPPEN IN A RELATIONSHIP WHEN TRUST IS LOST?

I was in university when I had my first long-term relationship. I trusted my then-boyfriend so much with everything. It so happened that intimacy boundaries were broken, and it caused me needless stress and uncertainty in my life. When I love, I love intensely. He was quick to anger, and yet I still forgave him for the many times that he caused me hurt and pain. After some time, I realized that the trust I had for him was being damaged little by little. As I looked back on those times, I came to realize that there were signs that we were in an unhealthy relationship, but I chose to overlook them. Mistakes are inevitable, but if your partner chooses not to admit and apologize for the mistakes that they did and puts the entire blame on you instead, take that as a warning sign. If your partner promises to support you on things that benefit your individual personal development, but his actions prevent you from growing and succeeding, take that also as a warning sign. It's not a healthy relationship if you can't trust your partner to actually be a partner in the things that matter to you.

Feelings of abandonment, anger, remorse, regret, and grief can all surface in a relationship when trust has been lost.

Trust issues in a relationship can rock us to our very core. Yet, if the personal relationship is fleeting or not very strong, most people move on.

We are all familiar with the sound of that nagging little voice that begins to whisper when something is off. You begin to have concerns in a relationship before you even discover a lack of trust. This uncertainty may gradually develop into mistrust, followed by fear and anxiety.

Finding the causes of the lack of trust in your relationship as soon as possible would be beneficial; else, fear may begin to set in. You would revert to acting defensively to defend yourself. It's only natural. This could cause you to distance yourself from your relationship or act out emotionally.

When distrust and fear set in, it is tough to think rationally about the causes of the lack of trust in your relationship. Neuroscientists have discovered that your brain shuts down when your fight-or-flight, or fear, response system is triggered. You are then naturally incapable of making sensible decisions.

All of this results in a tense or combative conversation that doesn't help in problem-solving. After all, having doubts about your partner's intentions is one of the major things contributing to a loss of trust in your relationship. Then, how do you decide which problems you should address?

When our defensive brain emphasizes all the negative things about our partner, blame often begins with that skepticism. It does a terrific job of protecting you, but it's not so excellent at realizing how untrustworthy your relationship is.

* * *

15 REASONS WHY YOUR RELATIONSHIP MAY HAVE TRUST ISSUES

It's disastrous when there is no trust in a relationship. It consumes you internally, and the worst part is that you're often too afraid to discuss it with the one person you ought to be able to confide in.

Understanding the main causes of the lack of trust in your relationship can help you determine what action to take next.

If you're looking for clarification, here are some potential answers to the question, "Why do I have trust issues?"

1. Childhood trauma

Although dealing with childhood trauma might be difficult, neither you nor your partner should lose trust in your relationship. We all enter into relationships with preconceived notions and worries about how to perceive the behavior of others. Our beliefs can occasionally be warped by events from our childhood.

For instance, you might not have grown up trusting your caregivers if you weren't given enough love and nurturing. Trust issues can be brought on by abusive childhoods or even an absent parent.

2. Abandonment issues

Fear of abandonment and even a lack of boundaries are other causes of trust issues. Group or individual therapy is often used to help people recover from those challenges. Of course, it's possible that your partner shares some of the same issues that are the root of your relationship's lack of trust.

3. Mismatched values

Being in a relationship with an individual who has a different outlook on life can make you lose trust in it. Of course, opposites attract, but over time you'll be able to tell whether your core principles are different.

According to studies, people who share values are more likely to feel a sense of shared identity and commitment, and feel fulfilled in a relationship. This makes it easier for them to have similar lives and complement one another. Contrarily, prioritizing different values quickly breeds mistrust.

One of the causes of your relationship's lack of trust is that your values don't align. In essence, you can't envision a future that you both share without having your values in line. Because of your disparate outlooks on life, there will inevitably be a lack of trust in your partnership or marriage.

4. Attachment style

Looking at our attachment style is often the first step in understanding the causes of the lack of trust in your relationship. We all relate to romantic partners in different ways, depending on whether they are secure or insecure.

When we were young, our caregivers taught us what a relationship looks like. According to this hypothesis, we apply these findings and presumptions to our adult relationships. Hence, if your father was emotionally absent, you might have a strong desire for intimacy and a need for constant reassurance.

Unfortunately, insecurely attached individuals often

attract one another. This is another cause of the lack of trust in your relationship.

In many situations, an anxious person will connect with an avoidant style person. Each of them recognizes something lacking in the other. It doesn't fill the void; it makes the first person more anxious and the second person more inclined to flee.

5. Unmet needs

One of the causes of people's possible lack of trust in their relationship is infidelity. Although it's easy to point the finger at such behavior, it's crucial to keep in mind that all behaviors have a source. Of course, this assumes that you aren't a serial cheater or a disturbed individual.

If the behavior is unusual, it can be the result of unmet needs. For instance, tensions can increase when one partner wants alone time while the other seeks intimacy. This may eventually drive people apart.

People are compelled to turn elsewhere if any of their requirements are not addressed by their work or home lives, which undermines the trust in their relationship.

If one partner doesn't feel they can openly share their needs, possibly because they will be held accountable or criticized, the trust issues may become even more problematic.

6. Unrealistic hopes

Relationships lacking trust may begin with erroneous assumptions or even the conviction that one of you is mentally telepathic. Maybe one partner expects the other to take care of them without even asking. Also, it may cause harmful inferences about how much or how little they truly care for you.

It makes sense that you can detect the telltale indications of a lack of trust in a relationship when so many thoughts are swirling about, and nothing definite is being said. Also, one of you might be harboring secret expectations of Hollywood or storybook perfection.

No relationship can live up to those standards, and this strain may also be a factor in why you don't trust your partner.

With time, control dynamics in a relationship can also shift. You might start to lose trust in a relationship if it diverges from your expectations. One partner may begin to doubt the motives of the other if they feel that they are being dominated by the other partner.

People can become insecure due to power struggles in a relationship, however it shouldn't be a competition between the two of you. You can be open, honest, and be yourself completely with each other in a healthy, balanced relationship.

External factors like changes in employment levels or if one person is significantly more senior than the other can sometimes lead to distrust.

When this is coupled with poor self-esteem, the "more junior" partner in the relationship may begin to feel left behind. They'll begin to doubt business conferences and phone conversations and make snap judgments.

Then all of a sudden, they want their partner to spend more time at home because they dislike their profession. The cycle of distrust therefore starts.

7. Toxic relationship

A toxic relationship you have with your partner may be the cause of a lack of trust in your relationship.

Insecure people often harbor doubts and are in toxic relationships. They encourage volatility, which hinders the development of a strong bond based on trust.

A toxic relationship is characterized by trust issues. It implies that the pair is unable to rely on one another and consistently questions the other's competence and behavior.

8. Dealing with social rejection

If you have experienced social rejection in the past, you might worry that it will happen to you again. This past social rejection may affect someone's behavior and personality over time.

You may begin to mistrust yourself and your partner or spouse out of a fear of social rejection. You live with the knowledge that your lover can leave you at any time. You might be unable to fully trust your lover because of this fear.

9. Issues with parents

You could struggle with trust if you lived in a chaotic household as a child.

Your perception of relationships and what can occur in a pair of individuals is permanently altered by the interaction between your parents.

You might come to distrust other people in your life if you were raised by parents who were distrustful of one another. Even if there isn't a valid reason, you might begin to suspect your partner of betraying you.

10. Lack of approval

Isn't it good to be appreciated by others? Don't you anticipate receiving compliments from your partner?

You may not form a connection with your partner if your
relationship lacks the affirmation that comes from acknowl-
edgment and compliments. You might have a hard time
trusting one another in these circumstances.

You begin to question their feelings for you and their acts
because of the lack of appreciation.

11. Increased complacency or neglect

It's a great mistake to take your partner for granted
because it can cause trust issues. Complacency can make you
question your partner's motives and feelings. It makes you
wonder if their commitment to the relationship or their
loyalty to you can be trusted.

Has your partner neglected you because of the pressures
of daily life? Or are you the one who neglected your relationship all along?

Usually, you want your partner to give you their full
attention and consideration. Without this genuine acknowl-
edgment, a person may feel unappreciated by their relationship.

Neglect makes it easier for doubts and insecurities to
invade your relationship. In a relationship that is either just
getting started or has been going on for a while, it could be
the cause of a lack of trust.

12. The need for control

You could desire control in your relationships and your
life.

Fear of getting hurt may be the core cause of a need for

control in a relationship, but it can also lead to a lack of trust.

The dominating partner's behavior displays a lack of confidence in their partner's intentions. Also, the partner develops mistrust since they feel like they can't be themselves around their dominating partner.

13. Fear of getting hurt

Don't let your anxieties dictate the dynamics of your relationship because they may lead to a lack of trust.

People may act in irrational ways out of fear of getting hurt. Due to their paranoia, they could begin to suspect their partner of certain things.

An unhappy relationship without trust might result from ongoing uncertainties and questions.

14. Untrustworthy behavior

The expectations you establish for your relationship are often based on your actions. It can reveal whether the relationship is lacking in trust.

You may mistrust your partner for acting recklessly and carelessly again if you have witnessed them doing so in the past.

It can be difficult to deal with a lack of trust in a relationship when it is the result of irresponsible behavior.

15. Jealousy

Trust is not fostered by jealousy. Instead, it depletes a relationship of it. It can be challenging for you to trust your partner when you are jealous of them.

In a jealous mood, you may regularly doubt your partner's behavior and motivations. This may be the reason you think of excuses not to believe someone.

SIGNS OF TRUST ISSUES

Determining if someone has trust issues or not might be difficult at times. Yet before you can take steps to address a problem, you must first recognize it.

When you can recognize the telltale indicators of distrust in a relationship, you can hunt for appropriate solutions.

The following are some typical signs of trust issues that you should watch out for:

1. Refusing to commit

Psychologists claim that people who struggle with trust also often struggle with commitment. This stems from a reluctance to be vulnerable and exposed because when there are trust issues, the prospect of a fulfilling relationship can seem improbable.

2. Believing that others are out to hurt you

Individuals with trust issues will also operate under the presumption that others are doing things to hurt them on purpose. It can be difficult to accept love gestures of compassion, admiration, or affection in general because you question whether they're genuine and not just a front for ulterior motives.

3. Cutting oneself off from other people

Many people with trust issues would withdraw at the first hint of trouble because of their presumptions and commitment phobia. When you don't trust people, developing new relationships becomes less crucial, and you can even decide to avoid them on purpose.

4. Being overly secretive about yourself

You may be extremely secretive about yourself when you do interact with people, especially those you are close to. The underlying sentiment behind this is often, "I'm afraid I can't be myself with you. That you won't accept me for who I am makes me nervous. Or I am afraid you won't let me in."

5. Starting arguments

We often become reactive and start arguments, even about little things, when we are suspicious and expect the worst. Consider the reactivity to be what can be seen above the waterline. When we believe our trust is being betrayed, trust issues fester beneath the surface and arise in big and small ways; it shapes who they are, and that impacts the relationship.

6. Being overprotective

You could feel overly attentive and protective of both yourself and the people close to you as a result of trust issues. If you think someone is trying to fool you, you might always be on the defensive, picture the worst-case situations in your relationships, or engage in catastrophic thinking.

7. Reluctance to communicate

Someone may find it hard to open up if they have trust issues. You may naturally begin to withdraw if something happens in the relationship when your identity isn't fully accepted or reflected back to you. Even if there has never been a reason for you to feel that way about a specific individual, you could fear that who you are won't be welcomed or valued.

HOW TO BUILD TRUST IN YOUR RELATIONSHIP

In order to establish trust, both the need to be trusted and to trust are crucial. That calls for shared effort and dedication. You must first understand one another's expectations as well as your own definitions of what trust implies. To increase trust in your relationship, try these strategies:

- Own up to your mistakes: Making mistakes is normal, but acknowledging them is harder. To build trust, you must first own your shortcomings. Avoid trying to hide your mistakes because doing so will just make things worse. Repentance demonstrates you want to foster mutual respect and trust.
- Forgive: Be willing to forgive one another when your partner admits to making a mistake. You should let go, accept, and focus on the "now" rather than holding on to prior arguments.
- Earn your trust: In every relationship, trust is not something that comes naturally. You must earn it by taking responsibility for your actions and behavior.
- Set an example: Act in a manner that your partner or spouse would appreciate. That's all there is to it.

Respect one another's personal values and act with honesty, responsibility, faithfulness, care, and compassion. All of these will persuade your partner to reciprocate.

- Actively listen: When your partner is speaking to you, listen without interrupting or passing judgment. They will also pay attention to what you have to say. This behavior creates the groundwork for developing trust.

- Keep your word: When you promise anything, be careful to follow through. Because breaking a promise is one of the simplest ways to lose trust, avoid making promises solely to appease your partner.

- Show interest: Demonstrate interest by becoming familiar with your partner's interests. Being curious, asking questions, and taking in the information will demonstrate your sincere interest. You will gain your partner or spouse's trust if they sense your sincerity.

- Be empathetic: Demonstrate empathy by understanding and meeting your partner's needs. Put yourself in their position to attempt to comprehend their issue. You may develop perspective and trust as a result.

- Communicate transparently: Speak honestly and openly, and avoid using text or the phone to discuss critical issues; instead, meet in person. Communications can be read incorrectly. Face-to-face communication is easier because you can read each other's emotions, intentions, and body language. The development of trust depends on effective communication.

- Mend rifts: As soon as a dispute arises, address it right away. Keep them from being brushed under the carpet and piled up. Put them to rest and move on.
- Dispel your doubts: Instead of waiting to ask your partner if you have any questions in your relationship, talk to them about it instead, as waiting could result in jealousy and arguments.
- Keep everything under wraps: Protect your privacy. Keep your information private, and don't let anyone in.
- Judge less and love more: Avoid judging or criticizing your partner. Instead, express your ideas in a positive way with the goal of fostering your partner's development. Without passing judgment, respect each other's differences.
- Encourage one another: In any relationship, encouraging one another is given. When you offer your partner moral and emotional support, they are more willing to try new things and take chances because they know they can rely on you for help.

* * *

Trust can occasionally make a person blind and open them up to deception. Yet, it is never too late to regain trust if you still want to be in the relationship or keep your partner.

CHAPTER 3: COMMUNICATION SKILLS FOR HEALTHY RELATIONSHIPS

*N*o romantic relationship can succeed if the two people cannot communicate well. Communication is known as the transmission, dissemination, and sharing of important information between two people. Living together as husband and wife, boyfriend and girlfriend, or in any other type of romantic partnership, can only be successful when there is an efficient information flow between the two parties. It is not surprising that many relationships end prematurely because of the weak foundation brought on by poor communication. As we are often taught, a successful relationship depends on excellent communication.

Strong communication and listening between two partners deepen the intimacy that acts as the glue that holds any relationship together. Similar to speaking, listening is a skill that people must work hard to develop. It is not something that comes naturally to everyone. Communication loses its purpose if we have a tendency to talk nonstop without listening while interacting with our partner on a regular basis. It is challenging to hear what your partner is saying when you interrupt or talk without listening, especially when our feelings, beliefs, and opinions will differ. All romantic relationships are made easier, sweeter, and more satisfying for both parties through effective communication. Lack of efficient communication can cause disagreements, frustrations, discontent, and conflict in any relationship, which can finally result in the breakup of the union.

KNOWING HOW IMPORTANT COMMUNICATION IS IN A RELATIONSHIP

Maintaining great communication in a relationship is important for a variety of reasons. The following three points will explain how improving our communication skills can strengthen our relationships.

1. It Demonstrates Value

It needs to be said that respect for the speaker is shown by paying attention to what they have to say. When conversing, paying attention to the other person demonstrates respect for what they have to say. Even if we disagree with what is being said, we should respect the opinions and emotions of the speaker. Effective communication allows you to express your values to your partner, who will then regard you as a valued asset. One partner becomes a liability to the other if there is ineffective or poor communication between them, and communicating becomes a duty rather than something you actually enjoy.

2. It Facilitates Understanding

Effective communication clearly differs from communication, and this distinction can be seen in effectiveness. Partners who communicate well can understand one another. Understanding should always be the ultimate purpose of communication; not to argue, not to dismiss, not to invalidate, but to understand. We can handle a crisis and take the required actions to improve the relationship when we tend to understand our partners and listen to them—even when we disagree. Knowing your relationship helps you prevent numerous issues, like frequent arguments, abusive language, harsh words to one another, and many more. Understanding your partner without passing judgment on them is a fantastic technique to win their devotion and adoration.

3. It Helps to Be Approachable

Knowing that someone is truly available to talk to us about anything can be helpful in relationships. Others may feel more at ease contacting us whenever they need or want to talk about anything that may be bothering them if we are able to communicate effectively. If we are approachable to our partners, our romantic relationships are more likely, to be honest, and fruitful. Many couples share a space but are unable to communicate with one another because their relationship lacks the level of familiarity that enables the discussion of even the most difficult topics.

Focusing on efficient communication as a crucial tool for developing and preserving your relationship is highly important. That's right – we want people to regard us, understand us, and be friendly toward us. Focus on developing your listening and communication skills in all areas, you will see how your romantic relationship develops as a result.

GOOD VS. POOR COMMUNICATION IN A RELATIONSHIP

Problem resolution and closeness are at the core of what separates excellent communication from poor communication. Poor communication exacerbates conflicts and drives partners further apart, while effective communication makes problems clear and fosters connections between partners.

Experts assert that individuals engage in effective communication when they:

- Pay attention and listen while your partner speaks
- Ask questions
- Affirm their partner's thoughts and feelings, especially when they differ from their own, by acknowledging and repeating back parts of what they have said.
- Listen to understand what your partner is saying instead of listening to respond.
- Don't shout at their partner

Meanwhile, those with poor communication skills may:

- Interrupt
- Act passive-aggressively
- Hold grudges
- Tiptoe around one another
- Guess or assume their partner's feelings
- Sweep issues under the rug rather than discuss them
- Argue over the same issue repeatedly
- Call their partner names

- Make threats
- Raise their voice.

In a relationship, being able to communicate effectively on a regular basis might make it easier for partners to deal with difficulties. Even in the midst of extremely stressful situations, good communication between partners can help partners defuse a crisis, maintain composure under pressure, utilize humor appropriately, apologize politely, and make the other partner feel heard and understood.

COMMUNICATION STYLES - AND HOW THEY AFFECT RELATIONSHIPS

Have you ever felt like you were moving in circles while having a conversation with someone? You made numerous attempts to communicate your point of view, but the other individual just wasn't clicking with you. It's possible that your communication style is less effective than you would think.

WHAT IS COMMUNICATION STYLE?

Your communication style is the way you engage and share information with others. A person's communication style, which includes their body language, facial expressions, and the deeper meaning or intention behind their words, can have a significant impact on the quality of their relationships.

Depending on the circumstance, the majority of people will occasionally employ all five communication styles, but they will typically revert to one "main" style. It's crucial to recognize not only your dominant communication style but also the styles of others around you as you seek to improve how you interact with others.

Although your primary communication style is founded on your upbringing and cultural influences, it is possible to switch from a less healthy communication style to an assertive one (an ideal style) with the support of a therapist and lots of practice.

Self-awareness is the first stage in identifying your communication style. What is your preferred communication style? Ask yourself honestly if you possess both the positive and negative characteristics of each style.

THE FIVE COMMUNICATION STYLES:

1. Assertive

It's usually regarded as the "best" style, yet it's also the least used. The assertive communicator has high self-esteem, the ability to strike a balance between being forceful and submissive, and the ability to effectively express requirements without hurting others.

Traits:

- Empathy
- Social awareness
- Self-protection, respect for others' needs and desires
- A direct manner of speaking
- An ability to take responsibility for one's own actions
- Emotional expression
- Open stance and eye contact.

- Speaks at a medium pitch, speed, and loudness
- People know where they stand with this individual

2. Aggressive

Achieving their goals often at the price of others, aggressive communicators are intent on winning and do not consider the feelings or needs of others.
  Traits:

- Believes that their opinions, needs, and feelings are more important than those of others
- Determined to succeed at all costs
- Bullying, intimidating, abrasive, and demanding
- Reacts out of fear and insecurity
- Emotionally explosive
- Threatening
- Interferes with other people's privacy when communicating
- Uses name-calling
- Shows superiority over others in posture and gestures
- People often feel defensive, resentful, or humiliated after speaking with them

3. Passive

Passive communicators always try to avoid conflict and think that other people's needs and wishes come before their own. They place a high emphasis on making people happy, yet they often find it difficult to speak up and contribute their thoughts.
  Traits:

- Apologizes for their ideas and opinions
- Avoids conflict
- Values "keeping the peace."
- Lacks confidence
- Feels like a victim
- Dishonest
- Submits to others' wishes and demands while ignoring their own
- Finds it difficult to accept responsibility for decisions
- When their unstated needs are not addressed, they could become resentful.
- Has a "small" presence
- Inexpressive
- Behaves submissively
- Often confuses others about what they want
- Speaks softly without making eye contact

4. Passively aggressive

Passive-aggressive communicators appear placid on the outside but conceal their genuine emotions and intentions because they feel powerless.

Traits:

- Acting angrily but subtly
- Venting their resentment by criticizing the target
- Whining
- Loves to gossip
- Cunning and sabotaging
- Patronizing and sarcastic
- Being two-faced – being kind to others' faces but aggressive behind their backs.

- They often adopt an asymmetrical posture, such as leaning, leaning with one leg out, or hands-on hip
- Pretends to be charming in their verbal expressions.
- People could feel bewildered, upset, or resentful after interacting with a passive-aggressive communicator.

5. Manipulative

Manipulative communicators are crafty and scheming individuals who are adept at managing and influencing others for their personal benefit while disguising their true agenda by acting as the victim.

Traits:

- Patronizing
- Calculated
- Using fake emotion to take advantage of others
- Asking for what they want in an indirect manner
- Controlling others through dishonest actions and words
- Making others feel sorry for them or obliged to help
- Using their facial expressions to convey sadness, helplessness, or self-pity.
- People are more likely to assist a manipulator out of guilt or obligation.

How to Get Better

The good news is that you can get better if you are connected with an unhealthy communication style and realize you need to learn how to be more assertive. Always keep in mind that you can only change yourself where communication is an issue. If you start speaking directly and empathically, it's likely that individuals around you will notice and adjust their tone as well.

- Give the other person plenty of time to speak while you listen. It takes effort to be receptive to debating opposing viewpoints. Remember that you are not compelled to agree with someone just because you listen to understand their viewpoint. Yet, it does convey to them your concern for them.
- Prioritize empathy, sincerity, and transparency in your communications. Be honest about your needs and wants, taking into consideration how they may influence the individual you are speaking to.
- Be self-aware and socially aware. Read between the lines (pay attention to body language, tone of voice, etc.) of the conversation. Pull back and let the other person know you understand and value their thoughts and feelings, even if you disagree if you notice them starting to become defensive.
- Use direct language and non-ambiguous body language. Don't leave the other person wondering what your true intentions are or what you really want. Focus on maintaining open body language and making eye contact.

WHY IS LISTENING IN A RELATIONSHIP IMPORTANT?

A good speaker must also be a good listener. By failing to pay attention to what others are saying and interjecting when they are speaking, you run the risk of misinterpreting a message. You need to be able to listen well if you want to communicate with your partner.

Listening is a skill that is developed in early childhood. The ability to listen varies from person to person. Even though it is hard to give everyone your full attention at all times, you may practice listening carefully. Without interrupting others, listen with the intent to understand rather than to react.

Any relationship's future is determined by the quality of listening.

WHAT IS ACTIVE LISTENING?

Active listening means being receptive to what others are saying. This strategy involves concentrating on what the other person is saying in order to understand their ideas, motivations, or standpoints. Making someone feel comfortable and appreciated will enable them to speak out when something essential needs to be discussed. This is the goal of active listening.

By engaging in active listening, you give the other person the opportunity to share their ideas, clarify a problem, or find a solution without judging or becoming emotionally involved. You can determine what needs to be done in a situation at the conclusion of a conversation. You can demonstrate active listening by:

- Making a variety of nonverbal cues or gestures to show that you are paying attention to what others are saying without cutting them off and preventing them from speaking.

- Rephrasing what someone else stated and making sure there are no misunderstandings.
- Making statements or offering recommendations by asking open-ended questions instead.
- Accepting as well as affirming the speaker's emotions rather than imposing your own opinions, judgments, beliefs, or sentiments.
- Starting a conversation by asking the other person if they want to talk or express themselves.

REFLECTIVE LISTENING: WHAT IS IT?

To help a speaker feel heard and understood, reflective listening involves paraphrasing what your partner or another person has said. Mutual understanding between the conversation's participants is necessary for effective communication. To foster mutual understanding in a discussion, reflective and active listening are both required.

To be understood as a listener, you must first understand the other speaker's (your partner's) point of view. To concentrate on your partner, you must set aside your opinions and feelings. This is a difficult undertaking since you can become defensive or eager to respond. You might utilize the following tips during reflective listening to help prevent any misunderstandings.

- When someone becomes defensive during a conversation, listen reflectively (with paraphrasing).
- Work on your reflective listening skills by paying close attention to your partner's words until you understand them.

- Be careful not to bring up your opinions or beliefs in the conversation.
- When expressing empathy or understanding during a conversation, use some neutral phrases.
- Reflect on the facts and your partner's thoughts, feelings, and desires in an effort to grasp what they are saying.
- Give up trying to be right.
- After you have fully understood what your partner is saying, express your opinions or ideas.
- Once you've come to an agreement, do what has to be done.

HOW TO LISTEN EFFECTIVELY

You can follow the tips below to learn how to listen actively:

1. Being present

When having a discussion, you must focus entirely on the speaker, which in this case is your partner. For instance:

- To prevent interruptions, you can keep your cell phone in "silent" mode.
- You can convey interest in the conversation through your body language by making eye contact with your partner or by leaning a little forward.
- You can demonstrate your interest in the subject.

2. Hold off on offering advice

Sometimes it makes more sense to talk through a problem than to try to "fix" it. You must learn to choose the appropriate moment to respond if you want to be a good listener. In some circumstances, it is preferable for a listener (you) to remain silent. Yet you must maintain eye contact with the speaker (your partner) and convey an interest in the dialogue through your body language.

3. Don't only listen to respond.

If you keep thinking about your response to something during a conversation, you will never learn to listen well. Instead of concentrating on how to react to your partner's words, your main goal when listening ought to be analyzing and understanding his or her thoughts.

4. Don't have an agenda

You must enter the dialogue with no preconceived notions. A competent listener will not intentionally steer the conversation in the direction of their choosing as they do not anticipate a specific result. If you'd like to be a good listener, you must let the other person (your partner) lead the conversation while responding in accordance with how they are feeling at the time.

5. Express interest

You must be interested in what your partner is saying if you want to learn how to listen well. Genuinely curious people who listen well do not interrupt to appear polite. They do so subtly, seeking clarification or learning more about the speaker(their partner) through their questions. If you act genuinely interested, your partner will be eager to talk and open up to you.

THE BENEFITS OF ACTIVE LISTENING IN RELATIONSHIPS

1. It Provides a Safe Space

Someone close to you, such as your partner, could wish to express their feelings or vent to you. Instead of opening up and trying to solve the problem, it is crucial in this situation to provide a safe space for them and allow them to share their opinions. You must engage in active listening and permit your partner to fully explain a situation. It makes it possible for them to solve a problem on their own. Exercises to build trust in the relationship for partners include listening to your partner's emotions, worries, and feelings. By doing this, you may make sure that your partner doesn't feel like they are being forced into a solution.

2. Improves Communication

By allowing you to concentrate on the feelings and experiences of your partner rather than preparing your next words, active listening can enhance communication. You keep an open mind throughout the conversation as a result. You can communicate effectively and understand the other person better.

3. Develops respect

You show respect for someone's ideas when you listen

carefully to them when they talk. When you provide respect to others, that is, your partner in this case, you'll earn their respect in return. Being attentive also demonstrates your respect for their viewpoints.

IMPORTANCE OF NONVERBAL COMMUNICATION IN RELATIONSHIPS

It is very easy to understand what nonverbal communication is. In relationships, nonverbal communication takes the form of positive or negative body language, keeping eye contact with the other person, expressions on your face, and other physical cues.

Relationships are built and maintained with the use of both verbal and nonverbal communication.

WHY IS IT IMPORTANT TO COMMUNICATE NON-VERBALLY?

Understanding the significance of nonverbal communication in a relationship can be vital for the survival of your marriage or relationship. Nonverbal communication in a relationship can be immensely reassuring.

A warm smile or a little touch on the arm are both examples of nonverbal cues that can help you and your significant other become closer.

Such interactions are crucial to the ability of two people in a relationship to connect with one another. Most times, we are unaware of how strong and important the unconscious mind is.

Your unconscious mind is most likely to notice things about other people, what they're doing, their behaviors, etc., even if they might not be that obvious.

Another example of nonverbal communication in a relationship is body language; a person's posture can reveal a lot about their thoughts. Some people are unable or unwilling to express their feelings. Identifying nonverbal signs can help a person understand what their partner is experiencing.

How to improve your nonverbal communication

Let's look at how nonverbal communication might be improved in love relationships.

Express your love and affection

One way to maintain a happy and healthy relationship is to tell your partner you love them. It's not required to say the three words "I love you" each time to accomplish that. In fact, you can show your love by making additional thoughtful and lovely acts.

As what we've already covered, nonverbal cues in a relationship include gestures, keeping eye contact, body language, and facial emotions. To maintain a healthy relationship, you must physically and non-sexually show your partner your affection.

Relationship problems may start if you can't "present" your feelings to your partner since they may believe you don't actually love them.

You can use typical, simple actions like holding their hands, massaging their shoulders while they watch TV, or even giving them an unexpected hug to express your love for them.

Pay attention to each other's emotional state

You and your partner must strive to be aware of one

another's feelings and moods in order to have a healthy relationship. Individuals often send out nonverbal signs about their emotions; and in order to grasp what's going on in their brains, you must be able to decipher these signals.

For instance, if they are making a lot of noise when doing the dishes, it may be your partner's way of communicating their anger to you.

Manage arguments well

No relationship is free from conflicts. You can, however, stop a dispute from developing into a full-fledged argument. Not only verbal communication, but also non-verbal communication is crucial.

Hence, when expressing yourself during a quarrel, it's often the nonverbal messages that you convey that can exaggerate the problem.

It is, therefore, preferable to keep a cheerful attitude during a disagreement. Making fists with your hands or whacking them against objects won't make things better for you.

Occasionally surprise them

You can surprise your partner with small gestures like preparing dinner, buying flowers, leaving kind messages for them to read, or simply performing your fair share of the household duties.

* * *

*Y*ou can express your emotions and devotion in a variety of ways without ever saying a word. This justifies the value of nonverbal communication.

That being the case, try out the relationship-related nonverbal cues stated above. Even though it could take some time to get things just right, with enough dedication, you'll be able to use both verbal and nonverbal communication to improve your relationship.

CHAPTER 4: SETTING BOUNDARIES AND RESPECTING EACH OTHER'S PRIVACY

*S*etting boundaries is essential to preserving a strong relationship with your partner, regardless of the type of relationship you have.

Your needs shouldn't have to collide with your desire for a close relationship. Being able to communicate successfully with your partner about your needs as an individual as well as a pair requires that you have a thorough awareness of who you are as an individual.

However, understanding your boundary issues and how to communicate them is not always easy.

This chapter offers advice on how to create healthy relationship boundaries to help you on your way to loving and therapeutic cohabitation.

WHAT ARE HEALTHY BOUNDARIES IN RELATIONSHIPS?

Respect for one another is created in relationships when healthy boundaries are present. Establishing boundaries enables us to understand what is anticipated in a relationship. Furthermore, boundaries teach us how to respect each other's limits, comfort zone, and personal space.

Every relationship has a different set of boundaries. We each have a distinctive relationship with our friends, coworkers, family, and romantic partners. For instance, you might not share financial information with your parents but you do with your romantic partner.

Similarly to this, you might show your family members a lot of emotion but not to your work colleagues. It's generally not suitable to discuss your relationship issues in the workplace. Yet, it's acceptable to express your frustration about your intramural soccer team's defeat.

No matter the relationship, we must accept pre-existing boundaries and give one another room to establish new ones. Both parties in a good relationship are capable of expressing vulnerability and setting limits, as well as having strong self-esteem. People are at liberty to feel, think, and act however they like.

Keep in mind that the limit is always set at the level of the person who is the least comfortable. For example in a group context, this person might be hesitant to speak up. Because of this, we often have certain social standards around settings like the workplace.

At the end of the day, everyone desires to be respected and cared for. You can get there by setting boundaries in your relationships, which enable you to express your wants and limitations.

WHY ARE RELATIONSHIP BOUNDARIES IMPORTANT?

Setting boundaries is a type of self-care. They serve as a means of protecting your mental well-being and making sure that your needs are honored.

For instance, understanding your partner's boundaries enables you to get to know them better overall. This is because if you respect their boundaries, they may feel more comfortable opening up to you. Genuine closeness and connection can then grow from there.

Growth in relationships can be challenging without clear boundaries. Everyone's mental health will improve if you speak up for yourself and give your partner a chance to do the same.

WHAT ARE THE 7 TYPES OF BOUNDARIES?

You need more than one or two boundaries in your relationship. There is no one-perfect boundary that can satisfy all of your desires. Consider the seven different types of relationship limits listed below as you start putting your comfort and capacity to function as an individual before anything else.

1. Physical Boundaries

Your right to privacy, to not be touched, and to fulfill basic needs (like sleeping or getting sustenance) are all protected by physical boundaries. You need to communicate to your partner what degree of physical contact, if any, is acceptable, how much privacy you require, and how to behave in your personal space. Your body and personal space are clearly defined by a physical boundary as being yours.

Examples:

- We don't keep or drink alcohol in our house.
- When someone sits too near to you, you walk away or say; I need a little more personal space.

2. Sexual Boundaries

The right to sexual consent, to request the kind of sex you want, and to be open about your partner's sexual past are all protected by sexual boundaries. They specify the type, frequency, timing, and location of the sex you desire.
Examples:

- I like to be caressed like this.
- I don't engage in sexual activity on first dates.

3. Mental or emotional boundaries

The right to have your own thoughts and feelings, to not have them judged or invalidated, and to not be required to consider the feelings of others are all protected by emotional or mental boundaries. Because emotional boundaries separate your feelings from those of other people, you are only liable for your own feelings and not for those of other people. By respecting one another's feelings and refraining from oversharing personal information that is unsuitable for the nature or degree of closeness in the relationship, emotional boundaries also help us to establish a sense of emotional safety.
Examples:

- I feel ashamed and helpless when you chastise me in front of our children. I'd like you to stop.
- I don't feel comfortable talking about it.

4. Religious or Spiritual Boundaries

Your right to practice your spiritual or religious views and to believe whatever you want is protected by spiritual boundaries.

Examples:

- Paul attends church alone because his partner doesn't share his beliefs
- I'm going to say a silent prayer before we eat.

5. Material and Financial Boundaries

The right to spend your money however you like, to not give or loan your money or possessions if you don't want to, and your right to earn money for a living are all protected by financial and material borders.

Examples:

- Please don't borrow my car without asking
- I'm on a budget, so let's stay in for dinner tonight; I'll cook.

6. Time Boundaries

Time boundaries safeguard how you use your time. They guard you against being overworked, being forced to do things you'd rather not do, and having people waste your time.

Examples:

- I set aside my evenings for family time. I'll reply to all emails for work first thing in the morning.
- Honey, this week I don't have time to take you shopping. I'll order some groceries from the grocery delivery service instead.

7. Uncompromising Boundaries

Uncompromising boundaries are deal-breakers that you definitely need to have in order to feel safe. They typically deal with safety-related issues such as physical violence, emotional abuse, drug or alcohol usage, fidelity, and serious medical conditions.

Examples:

- Infidelity is a deal-breaker for me, and I will not continue in this relationship if you cheat on me.
- I can't allow you to drive us in the car home when you've drunk too much. It's not only unsafe but also illegal.

We must be careful not to place too many of our boundaries in this category, even though we all need to have some non-negotiable ones. You must be prepared to stick to a non-negotiable boundary for it to have any significance. Setting uncompromising boundaries that you don't enforce is counterproductive.

UNHEALTHY BOUNDARIES

Often, unhealthy boundaries are either too rigid or too porous. Healthy individuals fall in the middle between these two extremes.

- Rigid boundaries isolate others, even close friends and family. Maybe you avoid discussing your feelings with your partner or seldom make time to hang out with friends.
- Porous or flimsy boundaries appear when you struggle to say "no" to people. You might, for instance, be overly eager to shoulder all the burdens of a relationship. Or perhaps you tend to talk too much when you're around strangers.

There are a variety of causes for people to struggle with unhealthy boundaries, including:

- A desire for power. Some people manipulate others by setting boundaries. A person might, for instance, utilize rigid boundaries to block communication and keep you from talking to them until they get their way.
- Fear of being rejected. You could be hesitant to share your emotions with your romantic partner if you're worried that they'll leave you because of your imperfections.
- A lack of prior experience with setting boundaries. Managing healthy boundaries can be difficult if you were raised in a community where bad personal boundaries were encouraged. Because your parents and siblings often invaded your

personal space, you may believe that doing so is acceptable.

- An overly compliant personality. If you try too hard to win people over, you might let them do things that are uncomfortable for you. Maybe you often take on more than you can handle or offer to help others out of a need for acceptance and love.
- Low self-esteem. You can believe that you lack a unique identity or that your needs and wants aren't important enough to express. Instead, you give importance to what others want. People, therefore, fail to notice your discomfort.

BOUNDARIES AND SUPPORTIVE BEHAVIOR

You might need to adjust your boundaries when, for example, your partner is struggling with addiction in order to prevent supporting their bad conduct. When you protect someone from the repercussions of their behavior, you are enabling them. For instance, you might want to offer to fund their legal expenses if they were arrested for DUI or lie to others to hide signs of a gambling or drug addiction. While you may think these behaviors are helpful at the time, in reality, you are hindering your loved one from learning from their mistakes.

Addiction-related circumstances are not the only ones where enabling is used. Some mental health conditions may also experience it. For instance, if a loved one suffers from a social anxiety disorder, you can try to protect them from awkward situations by advocating for them in public. As a result, they don't resolve the problem on their own and instead continue to rely on you.

SUFFOCATION IN RELATIONSHIPS & HOW TO PREVENT IT

A relationship is suffocating when it starts to feel like a burden or when you start to resent your partner for taking all of your time, using up all of your energy, and having unrealistic expectations.

TEN INDICATORS THAT A RELATIONSHIP IS SUFFOCATING YOU

You should pay attention to these warning signs:

1. Your partner needs you or clings to the relationship.

Clingy partners are unhappy and irritable unless they receive continual nurturing from you to acknowledge and meet needs consistently.

They typically just get one-sided attention from you and spend little time supporting you. This person is self-centered but wants you to be compassionate toward them.

2. The nature of the relationship is being manipulated.

Manipulating a partner is a preferred strategy to acquire what they want when they are being smothered in a relationship.

When a partner feels smothered in a relationship, they may claim that they don't see you often enough or that you don't try to spend "quality" time with them while, in reality, they consume your every waking moment.

Some manipulators will pretend to be ill in order to keep you from interacting with loved ones or friends or from taking advantage of the time alone.

3. Owning a space of your own is not an option.

A partner that just shows up at the worst possible time and assumes they can fit into your schedule is not considerate of your personal space.

For instance, if you want to participate in a friends' night or a certain organized activity or personal appointment but your partner suddenly interrupts the event, despite your wish to do so on your own, this raises the red flag that your relationship is suffocating you.

4. The amount of daily contact has become excessive.

The only time you can get away from your clinging companion is when you both leave for work for the day. Unfortunately, multiple calls and texts are made to keep you focused on them throughout even this respite.

A lot of affection and physical touch at first could seem somewhat expected, given the newness and the need to get to know one another. Yet, having to recount your day's activities minute by minute might get tiresome and irritating after a while.

5. The jealousy is almost insane.

If you're not very careful, toxicity could appear in this case. Unreasonably jealous partners obsess over who you hang out with when you're not with them.

Depending on the individual, it may cause your partner to feel uneasy and upset as they wonder if your affections for them are sincere.

6. Lying starts to become the norm for you

When you feel trapped in a relationship, you may actively look for ways to avoid spending time with your partner.

Instead of bringing happiness or fulfillment, the concept causes irritation and unhappiness. You might even discover that you need to lie to have a few hours alone or to spend time with relatives or friends.

7. Efforts to influence you

Some partners who take over their partner's life eventually try to change things by crossing personal boundaries.

They may not be obvious at first, but over time, they will become overt and intrusive, such as when someone buys you clothes based on what they believe your sense of style should be or rearranges the furniture in your home.

Such actions go beyond the telltale indicators of being suffocated in a relationship and instead result in control.

8. You don't feel comfortable speaking your views or expressing yourself.

Everyone has a right to express their opinions. It's tremendously stifling and a terrible scenario to be a part of when opinions are suppressed to the point where you don't feel free to speak your mind or express how you feel about almost any issue, including the relationship.

Again, this creates toxicity and is unhealthy; therefore, no one should feel as though they must internalize their emotions in order to please someone else.

9. Your private life has become public

Social media is a useful resource. But whether you want

your private life to be made public or not, you will see yourself all over your partner's social media sites if you feel trapped in a relationship with someone who is too clingy.

It can include highly private moments when you're not aware, arguments you have when your partner decides to consult friends for advice, or photos from your most recent date.

10. Your lover has made you the focus of their universe.

If your partner stops making plans with friends, spending time with relatives, or genuinely engaging in any activity that doesn't involve you after even a short while, the relationship becomes suffocating.

Instead of seeing the need to maintain healthy personal lives outside of the relationship, your partner has chosen to spend every waking hour together as a couple.

SETTING AND MAINTAINING BOUNDARIES

While it's typically advisable to start creating boundaries early on in a relationship, doing so can help a relationship grow at any point.

In many circumstances, it takes getting to know each other more to recognize that a particular boundary is necessary. For instance, it could take some time for you to understand that the highly frequent texts from your partner causes you to become distracted while at work or that a romantic interest looks overbearing.

If you are having problems connecting or talking with a person in your life, the following tips can help you set boundaries.

Tip 1: Be aware of your relationship goals.

It can be challenging to get your needs satisfied in a relationship, whether it be romantic or platonic if you don't know what they are. Consider your principles and beliefs as a starting point.

Consider asking yourself:

- What qualities do I like to see in other relationships?
- What actions irritate me?
- What traits in others do I find admirable?
- What material things are most important to me, and why?
- What activities do I enjoy doing?
- What gives me satisfaction?

You can start to envision the kinds of boundaries you require by developing a deeper awareness of who you are. If you are aware of how much independence means to you, you should probably establish financial boundaries with your partner. You might also establish physical boundaries if you value privacy even when out in public.

EVALUATING YOUR RELATIONSHIP WITH SOMEONE

You can also figure out what boundaries you require by considering how other people make you feel. Asking yourself questions will help you consider your feelings after interacting with others.

- Did you feel disrespected by the other person's jokes or remarks?

- Did they engage in any behavior that put you in danger or physical discomfort, such as raising their voice angrily?
- Did you experience pressure to act in a way that didn't align with your values?
- Did the person's wishes or expectations of you leave you feeling overburdened?
- Did you feel that they were abusing your sense of control or treating you like a child?

A moment of reflection can help you decide whether you need to create boundaries with the individual moving forward.

Tip 2: Discuss your needs with the individual.

It's crucial to understand how to express your wants to people clearly. In family settings, family members may find it more difficult to understand and abide by your ground rules as a result of hurried interactions, awkward language, and ambiguous requests.

- Think about timing. The greatest time to establish boundaries with your partner or spouse is when you both feel at ease and can concentrate on the talk. Try to calm yourself and then return to the conversation if you're in the middle of an argument.
- Be organized. Are you afraid to express your needs? Before the conversation, make a list of your points so that you can express them effectively.
- Think about the delivery. To communicate your feelings, try to employ "I" statements. Avoid using

the word "you," which might be accusing. As an illustration, you might say, "I felt overwhelmed by the quantity of work I had to handle while you were away." Laying the foundation for a relationship boundary by expressing your emotions is a terrific place to start.

- Be precise. You may convey the idea by just saying, "I'd want more personal space," but it's preferable to be as explicit as possible to avoid upsetting the other person. Try something like, "I feel insulted and uncomfortable when you enter my room or when I'm in the bathroom without asking. Please knock before you do. The other person will understand that you are serious but not disrespectful if you speak in a calm but forceful tone.

- Address feedback. The boundaries will determine whether your companion asks you questions or not. Although you don't have to justify your requirements or explain yourself, doing so could help the other person see things from your perspective. To make sure the correct message was delivered, you might even ask follow-up questions.

FEEDBACK IN ROMANTIC RELATIONSHIPS

It's especially crucial in love relationships to directly ask your partner how they feel about a request rather than assuming. Find out if they think it's unfair or uncommon. Or inquire as to if it interferes with whatever they require or desire.

Both of you are responsible for putting your own

thoughts and feelings into words so that they can be understood.

Let others be responsible for their feelings. We often have a natural inclination to be concerned with how others see us and respond to our words and deeds. However, you shouldn't hold yourself accountable for how the other person responds to the boundaries. For instance, they might object if you ask for extra "me time." You might feel selfish or guilty as a result of this. Recall the primary reason you're placing the boundaries: To indulge in your separate interests and prevent feeling overly crowded emotionally, you want some time to yourself. Do not feel that you must ignore your own needs.

Tip 3: Maintain boundaries

Not everyone in your life will always abide by your boundaries. One could unintentionally be crossed by a partner or purposefully by problematic family members.

State your needs again. It's possible that the other individual misunderstood or simply forgot your initial request. Be lucid, assertive, and cool when expressing your needs.

Establish clear and fair consequences for crossing a line. For instance, if someone often talks over you, you could respond with something like, "I feel disrespected when you talk over me. I'll have to stop talking to you if you do that again.

Only list consequences that you intend to enforce. The other person will feel empowered to push your boundaries in the future if you don't follow through on a consequence. For instance, it's crucial to follow through when you threaten to leave a relationship with your partner if they continue to lie to you.

CHAPTER 5: DEALING WITH CONFLICT IN A POSITIVE WAY

*A*lmost all relationships will inevitably experience conflict. It may also be a major cause of relationship problems or stress. Hence, developing conflict resolution skills is crucial. Unfortunately, keeping quiet when upset is not a wise long-term strategy, despite the fact that many people do so.

Unresolved conflicts can lead to resentment and unsolved arguments in the relationship. Even more significant, continuous fighting may potentially harm your health and lifespan.

Unfortunately, resolving disputes can also be challenging. Attempts at conflict resolution might worsen a conflict if they are handled improperly.

This chapter discusses conflict resolution strategies that can be used in intimate relationships as well as other environments where conflict may occur.

Here are some principles to make conflict resolution easier and less stressful for individuals who weren't raised in a family where excellent conflict resolution skills were always modeled (and, let's face it, how many of us were?).

RELATIONSHIP CONFLICTS: WHAT ARE THEY?

Conflicts in a relationship include differences of opinion, discussions, fights, and battles between two people.

Relationship conflict is common. You two couldn't possibly agree on everything and never disagree. When handled properly, conflicts in a relationship might even make your relationship or marriage stronger.

The way you handle difficulty in a relationship, not the conflict itself, is what may make or break it.

Hence, it's important to understand what causes conflict in one relationship before we discuss the different forms of relationship issues and how to handle them.

WHAT ARE THE CAUSES OF RELATIONSHIP CONFLICTS?

You and your partner are quite different individuals who just so happen to be in love. You start to understand each other better as your relationship develops.

You learn about one another's annoyances, and try to understand one another's perspectives and much more. Below are some of the causes that contribute to conflict starting to emerge in your relationship.

1. Wrong expectations

When someone's expectations aren't satisfied, it's one of the main reasons why a relationship becomes tense.

This happens when someone begins to develop expectations. Expectations are common, but occasionally they become excessive. Naturally, this will lead to problems in their relationship.

One begins to feel resentful at their partner for not being able to "get" what they want or need, but they often forget that no one can read minds.

For instance:

At your high school reunion, all of your friends are present with their partners. You've been discussing this with your partner for several months, and you were expecting him to be your date, but he canceled due to a meeting.

You experience pain and unlove. After all, you anticipate that he will leave his meeting and opt to prioritize you over his business. Because your expectations weren't satisfied, you now perceive something conflicted in your relationship.

2. Being egocentric

We occasionally lose sight of the fact that we are in a relationship because we are too preoccupied with what we want and what we believe to be right.

How do we interpret this?

It implies that you must cooperate with your partner when you're in a relationship. You and your partner should collaborate on everything, from making decisions to spending money on groceries.

Unfortunately, it happens a lot. When making decisions, someone in the relationship is unable to consider how the other person might feel. Selfishness is the main reason relationships break down.

For instance, you believe it would be ideal to relocate to a city where you can realize your aspirations. Nevertheless, you forget to realize that your partner will need to leave their aging parents in the small town. A conflict may arise between you two if your partner starts to go against your plan.

3. Ineffective communication

Most articles discuss how important communication is to a relationship. Also, a lack of it can lead to a variety of conflicts in relationships.

Condescending language, screaming, and sarcasm when communicating can lead to conflict and further deteriorate the connection. As the saying goes, it's not what you want to say that matters; it's how you say it.

For instance:

You and your partner can't decide whether to enroll your children in a private or public school. Nevertheless, instead of talking it through with each other, you both start insulting each other. You start yelling and bringing up previous arguments.

You end up arguing rather than understanding each other's ideas and coming to an agreement.

4. Resentfulness

Relationship conflicts can arise when, for example, your partner cracks an offensive joke, makes a decision on their own without consulting you, or leaves you feeling neglected.

Many of these unpleasant feelings fester and turn into resentments when you fail to connect with each other and share the things that may have hurt you.

Your heart is gradually becoming increasingly painful and unsatisfied, and you are always ready to let it all out.

For instance:

Finally, your partner received his first paycheck! Because you want to go on a lavish date, you are overjoyed. You thought he knew what you meant when you mentioned a neighboring restaurant to him.

Though he didn't, not even a gift was given to you by him. You might become resentful of your partner as a result of this circumstance.

5. Criticism that is unwarranted and finger pointing

Conflicts can take many different forms when everything that happens is somehow your fault.

Who wants to stay in a relationship with someone who is continuously critical of their choices? It's like blaming someone else while avoiding taking responsibility. This mindset can eventually lead to problems in your relationship.

For instance, when selecting the best brand of air conditioner for the home you have together, you present your case and recommend the brand you prefer. The AC unit, however, experienced problems when it arrived. As a result of this, your partner then lashes out at you for making bad choices.

TYPES OF RELATIONSHIP CONFLICT

Now that you know various reasons for relationship conflict, it is time to understand the five basic types of relationship conflict. What are the various forms of conflict that can arise in relationships?

1. Kids

One of life's greatest joys is becoming a parent, but for some couples, this may also lead to conflict if you and your partner aren't prepared for the burden.

The two of you might disagree on whether it's preferable to start a family now or wait until you are both financially stable, or to not have any children at all. There may be numerous topics to address in this situation, which may result in conflict.

2. Money

Among all kinds of conflicts, disagreements over money are among the most common ones that separate relationships and marriages.

In a relationship, when two people decide to live together, they must talk about their financial situation. You will learn how your partner manages their finances at this point. The truth is that not every couple views money in the same way.

Finding out that your partner is a big spender or has outstanding loans might already be a source of contention. A common occurrence is when a hard-working partner begins to harbor anger toward the other who is financially irresponsible.

Imagine doing everything you can to save for the future, only to learn that your partner has bought an expensive item that you don't even need. These kinds of problems often never get handled and lead to breakups.

3. Intimacy

When a relationship first starts or when in the honeymoon phase of relationships, couples enjoy being physically intimate; and in the context of marriage and long-term partnerships specifically, being sexually intimate. Nonetheless, the desire to engage in expressions of physical intimacy may diminish as the relationship develops.

What causes this to happen?

You and your partner may have different sexual desires as a result of your hectic schedule, stress, domestic duties, low self-esteem, and even children.

Wouldn't it damage your feelings if, despite your best efforts to make love and be intimate with your partner or spouse, they instead give you a frustrated expression and make excuses about how busy and worn out they are?

While one desires intimacy and sexual contact, the other tries to decline and withdraw. The relationship may suffer if the pair doesn't discuss this or deal with the problem because it may lead to conflict.

4. Household responsibility

What conflicts specifically lead to a partner's final separation? When one of you does all the domestic chores, and the other doesn't give a damn, this might lead to animosity building up within one partner.

Even if you both work, you are the only one who cleans and takes care of all the domestic chores. To top it off, your partner would expect you to handle everything while carelessly leaving all of their filthy dishes in the sink, or clothes on the floor.

Nobody wants to continue in a relationship like this. If you don't deal with the problem, your resentment can build up.

5. Jealousy

Jealousy is bred by insecurity. This is the form of relationship conflict that causes the most harm. One partner has a tendency to fabricate problems that aren't even there if they feel uneasy about the relationship and their partner. Unfounded suspicions and conflicts might develop from intrusive thoughts.

The harm that insecurity may do is immense. For instance, you can begin to suspect your partner of being unfaithful. You then start to envision instances of adultery. Before you realize it, you are cultivating bitterness and anger over unfounded assumptions.

Any kind of phone call or embrace from a person your partner knows can already set off an outburst, which not only leads to conflict but also has the potential to break up your relationship.

EIGHT DESTRUCTIVE ACTIONS TO AVOID WHILE IN A RELATIONSHIP CONFLICT

Most people have experienced acting unreasonably in a relationship, particularly during a fight or a disagreement. Despite the fact that disagreement is healthy and can sometimes be a natural component of an intimate relationship, it requires some ability and effort to be productive and constructive during times of conflict and detachment.

People don't like to engage in damaging actions. People often express to me how terrible they feel about how they behave when they are at odds with their partner. Nonetheless, the majority of people feel helpless or unsure of how to break the cycle. They sense a desire to defend themselves because they feel intimidated, hurt, agitated, and/or enraged.

In a conflict, when both partners react, a vicious cycle of negativity is started. This negativity may fester and develop into a challenging pattern. Usually, both partners are caught in a vicious cycle of hurt, rage, and reaction. These cycles cause a lot of disconnection, discontent, and separation over time in the relationship.

Staying the same while hoping that your partner will change will not result in change. We often say to each other, "No, you go first," while waiting for our partner to make a change. I've witnessed long-lasting "stand-offs" between partners that don't work out. Start with YOU, the only thing you can control. Do your best. It will have an impact. When one person changes, the entire dynamic of the relationship is changed.

The most significant thing to do is to confront any of these nine damaging behaviors to prevent relationship conflict as soon as you notice them. Relying on harmful actions will have very few positive effects. Instead, I urge you to devote your time and effort to handling conflict in a productive manner. Even though it could be a challenging undertaking, it will be well worth the time and money. I encourage you to read through this list with the goal of learning.

1. Personal attacks or name-calling

This is the first example of actions to avoid a relationship conflict. When someone uses disrespectful and offensive language toward another individual, this is known as name-calling. Name-calling is a word used with the goal of criticizing, accusing, rejecting, shaming, ridiculing, or condemning another person. These words could include terms like "jerk," "loser," "selfish, domineering, inconsiderate, jealous, rude, and harsh," "narcissistic," "crazy," "irrational," "childish," and "immature," among others.

Name-calling and character attacks are similar, but character attacks target someone's character more broadly. What you disagree with is your partner's personality, traits, intents, family, race, religion, beliefs, etc., not what they are saying.

Avoid using all-or-nothing language when calling someone names or attacking their character in a relationship (e.g., "you always" or "you never"). Your partner will most likely defend themselves against character attacks and respond to your generalization by attempting to present evidence that refutes it. This will divert attention from your concern and lead to a discussion about whether your partner is "always or never" or anything which is unrelated to the problem. This back-and-forth often turns into a heated argument. It is more probable that they will be able to concentrate on what you are saying rather than defending against your broad generalization if you use language that is more flexible or highly particular (e.g., "it seems as though you occasionally..." "in this instance, you...").

2. Dismissive body language

This is the second example of actions to abstain from during a relationship conflict. These are actions or nonverbal cues used to put down, degrade, or reject your partner. A few common physical gestures include waving a finger, putting a hand up, making a shooing motion with the hand, hand yapping, spinning around to face your partner, sighing heavily, seeming disengaged and distracted, shaking your head "no" when your partner is speaking, and raising an eyebrow. A dismissive body language can occasionally be more hurtful than a verbal assault. It often suggests a desire to outdo your partner.

Be mindful of your facial expressions and body language if you can. Have an open mind and try to remain impartial.

3. Silent Treatment

This is the third example of actions to avoid a relationship conflict. Silent treatment includes shutting down, ignoring, avoiding, and/or refusing to answer your partner's questions or comments. Neglecting to talk about or debate certain subjects that your partner may bring up is another example. In general, silent treatment causes greater hurt and pain. The ignored partner often feels despised and disrespected. There is no resolution while doing the silent treatment. The negative cycle is exacerbated when partners employ silent treatment to chastise or communicate disapproval.

Communicate gently that you are not ready to talk if you are too hurt or angry to do so. You may even go so far as to offer a time that you would be available to check-in.

4. Assuming

Assumption is the fourth example of actions to avoid a relationship conflict. It is the act of assuming or choosing what your partner is thinking and feeling without their knowledge or consent. Another way to assume is by mind reading. Sadly, this is a very, very common practice. On the one hand, when we are very close to someone, we will watch them and try to understand their motivations and why they act the way they do. It will be natural for us to assume certain things about their behavior and have certain expectations from them. On the other hand, especially during a disagreement, we often get it wrong because we don't truly understand what they are feeling or thinking. Many times, people assume they understand what their partner is thinking or feeling, only to discover that their understanding is incorrect. Mind reading and assumptions often result in misunderstandings and hurt feelings.

In theory, the solution is rather simple. Acknowledge that you haven't asked your partner about their thoughts, behaviors, or desires or gotten any information about them. Recognize that your perception of the world is based on assumptions or fantasy. After that, have your partner confirm your assumption.

5. Trying to be right

This is the fifth example of actions to avoid a relationship conflict. It is typical for one or both parties to switch during a disagreement from the stance of "trying to resolve an issue" to the one of "trying to be right." In other words, couples will start a conversation with the aim of productively discussing a problem only to become sidetracked and argue about whose reality is true. Couples will feel pitted against one another, needing to defend their positions and having the option of winning or losing. This defines a one-up, one-down power structure in which only one individual may succeed or be right.

Reaching a conclusion, understanding, and a mutually beneficial solution are no longer the goals if the goal is to win. It is quite challenging to maintain a polite and compassionate position with one another when partners lose sight of their objectives.

Try to see the value in your partner being honest, open, and real, even if they are expressing a different point of view.

Their opposing viewpoint does not constitute an insult to you or a denial of your point of view.

6. Being defensive

This is the sixth example of actions to steer clear of during a relationship conflict. When they feel on guard, people tend to become defensive most of the time. They believe they are being attacked or are anticipating criticism. Those who are on the defensive will avoid taking responsibility, avoid doing anything wrong, and refuse to examine their own behavior. They are less interested in listening honestly and unbiasedly than they are in defending or protecting themselves. An extremely defensive partner often makes their partner feel unheard and ununderstood. Unresolved problems will go neglected, and the dispute will intensify.

Being defensive can take many different shapes, but it typically involves trying to challenge or contradict your partner's viewpoint. Contradicting or accepting the opposing argument are two ways to achieve this. Being defensive can include engaging in "devil's advocate" tactics, pointing out mistakes, or presenting counterarguments with solid data. In essence, it involves assuming an adversarial attitude and diffusing what your partner is saying or doing with regard to a specific issue or situation.

Give your partner your whole attention if you can. Even if you disagree, stick with your partner's point of view when you feel defensive. Try to see yourself in their shoes. Consider yourself in their position.

7. Control tactics

This is the seventh example of actions to avoid a relationship conflict. The use of various ways to try to influence or dominate a situation or a person is known as a control tactic. These tactics may include talking over or interrupting the other person, making demands or threats, giving deadlines, or trying to steer the topic. When someone feels hopeless, helpless, or afraid, they turn to control tactics. Oftentimes, those who try to dominate others are unaware that they are doing so. In essence, they are grabbing at their partner in an effort to calm their own fear and worry.

The feeling of separation and isolation from your lover can be very frightening. Because you currently sense the loss of the emotional relationship and connection, it could even feel like you are losing your partner. Although this detachment may seem dangerous, the more you try to control your relationship, the more they will distance themselves from you. Remember that your partner is resisting your attempts to exert control over them in this situation (not you).

It is more probable that your partner will lean towards connection with you if you can deal with the anxiety and risk of momentary disconnect and upset, as well as try to understand their feelings and experience (no matter how terrifying it may appear to you). Although it seems quite counterintuitive, this often results from giving up on trying to control everything.

8. Anger outbursts

Anger is the eighth and last example of actions to abstain from during a relationship conflict. The act of expressing anger, often abruptly and uncontrollably, is referred to as an outburst of anger. Sarcasm or passive-aggressive behavior are examples of smaller-scale ways that anger might be expressed. Alternatively, anger might be conveyed more forcefully, such as by throwing, punching, slamming, or shattering things. When someone is "at their wit's end" or has had their "last straw," they are often beyond their threshold of what they can tolerate and experience an outburst of wrath. Often, the person who is angry believes that their partner is intentionally upsetting them or trying to hurt them, and they transform it into a matter of justice, fairness, and principle.

Typically, the receiving partner experiences hurt, fear, and worry. The feeling of safety and security may be threatened by the outbursts. Anger outbursts don't lead to resolution or repair. Trying to hurt your partner on purpose can be extremely destructive and even violent.

If you have a tendency to lose your temper or get angry easily, I would strongly advise familiarizing yourself with some anger management techniques. In that way, you will know how to show your anger in a healthy way and find strategies to defuse potentially explosive situations. Anger is a good human emotion. Anger lets us know when there has been wrongdoing, injustice or when a line has been crossed. When someone feels insulted, embarrassed, or provoked, anger may also come to the surface. The manner someone expresses their anger determines whether it will be positive or negative.

SUGGESTIONS FOR MANAGING CONFLICTS IN YOUR RELATIONSHIP

Every relationship will experience conflict at some point, but how they are handled is what counts. Here are some suggestions to bear in mind that will help you handle your next conflict in a healthy manner. How you handle a problem with your partner can influence whether your relationship is healthy or unhealthy.

1. Provide a friendly atmosphere that encourages open discussion.

You and your partner can talk openly about what is upsetting you and what is working well in your relationship if it is healthy. In order to prevent anyone from feeling like they are doing everything wrong, it is crucial to discuss both the positive aspects of the relationship as well as the issues. A clue that your relationship can be unhealthy is if you feel that you can't communicate honestly about significant concerns, such as life issues, money, aspirations, and anything that affects or worries you on a larger scale. If you are unable to express your emotions without worrying about your partner's reprisal or them being too irritated and defensive, you may be in an unhealthy or abusive relationship.

2. Be cool in heated conversations and treat everyone with respect.

Keep your insults to a minimum toward your partner. Maintain the conflict's attention on the pertinent matter; refrain from interjecting insults and slurs about the other person. Also, if your partner often becomes agitated, hostile, or begins cursing, these are indications that your relationship can be abusive. No one should yell at you, curse at you, or otherwise make you feel uneasy or afraid when you are arguing, regardless of what sparked the conflict. You shouldn't ever feel threatened, or like you need to be cautious so as not to aggravate your partner further.

3. Locate the source of the issue.

There are occasions when disagreements with your partner are the result of unmet demands. Take time to determine whether there is a bigger problem at play if it looks like your partner is worrying over trivial things. For instance, for university students, if your partner is concerned about your ability to maintain your grades or is irritated that you are partying in the middle of the week, they may want you to set aside more time for your relationship. Think about the situation from your partner's perspective and consider how you would feel if the positions were reversed. Instead of merely trying to get your message over, be considerate of your partner.

4. Be wary of arguments that are motivated by a desire for control.

It is a HUGE red flag if you suspect that your partner is trying to restrict what you do. If your partner gets upset when you text other people, doesn't like it when you put work and responsibility before them, pressures you to hook up with them, or attempts to limit your time with friends, these are all indications that they might be trying to exert control over you. Even if they try to excuse it by stating that "I'm just over-protective," "it's my trust issues," or "it's because I love you," no one should ever try to control you, especially not your partner. If any of these actions ring a bell in your relationship, you should get help right now.

5. Try to find a middle ground.

It's crucial to strike a balance between what each partner

wants and feels comfortable doing. You will reach an understanding of issues without feeling as like you are making significant compromises for your relationship if you both want to make it work. Conflict resolution often involves making compromises, and it might be easier than you think to reach a middle ground! If you and your partner are fighting over seeing your friends or your partner's friends, alternate days to spend time with each friend group or spend a night alone. Ask your partner to contribute the next time you go grocery shopping if you feel like they are constantly devouring all of your food.

6. Choose your battles wisely and agree to disagree.

Sometimes it's important to question whether the issue at hand is indeed worth fighting over. Is it just about what to eat for dinner? Using the same covers while sleeping? What should be your upcoming Netflix binge? Sometimes it's best to just ignore a little issue. It probably isn't worth your energy if you won't still be upset about it the following week. You won't always agree with your partner, so if you believe the disagreement is too significant to ignore, you should ask yourself whether you two are truly compatible.

7. Think about whether or not the problem can be fixed.

Sometimes we fight with our partners over REALLY important issues that affect our lives, such as whether to buy or rent a home, work/study full-time or part-time, whether to have children, where to reside after graduation, or other examples applicable to your stage in life. Consider whether the relationship is truly worthwhile if you believe that you will have to compromise your ideals, principles, or aspirations in order for it to function. You and your partner need to share the same perspective on the broader picture for your relationship to work. One of the key components of compatibility is sharing similar values, views, and dreams with the other person.

* * *

*W*hen problems arise, try to refrain from immediately resorting to fighting. Couples who want to resolve relationship issues without hurting each other's feelings must remember to keep the lines of communication open. Learning to listen, remaining polite, trying to understand your partner's point of view, and forgiving one another are all part of the effective communication that we talked about in Chapter 3.

You'll be able to resolve conflicts in the future in a healthy and beneficial manner if you keep these suggestions in mind when you have your next argument. Even if it means you get to turn into birds together in the end, nobody wants to be like Noah and Allie from The Notebook, who never agree on anything and fight all the time. *(Side note - I love this Nicholas Sparks book and movie, except for the parts that are questionable.)* The goal we have here is to be able to handle conflicts that arise in a constructive way.

CHAPTER 6: THE IMPORTANCE OF SELF-CARE IN RELATIONSHIPS

*I*t's crucial to prioritize taking care of yourself in your daily life. Self-care involves prioritizing and caring for your mental, physical, and emotional health. Simultaneously, it's important to take care of yourself in a relationship, but this might often look a little different than self-care for a single individual. Relationship self-care refers to the delicate balancing act of caring for yourself when you are in a committed relationship in order to have the greatest relationship possible.

It may often be challenging to take time for yourself without seeming conceited or demanding, especially when you're in a relationship. Yet regardless of your relationship state, self-care is crucial. Self-care will make you and your partner more accepting, loving, and understanding of one another, which will reflect in your relationship. Two healthy people are necessary for a healthy partnership. Only you are capable of managing your mental, physical, and emotional well-being, but doing so can be quite difficult, especially if you have another person (your partner) on your mind.

You tell people how to treat you, not the other way around. Taking the greatest possible care of yourself is the best lesson you can teach them. Self-care is not being selfish.

In reality, it is essential to choose a strategy that complements your uniqueness and personality because doing so will support the maintenance of your physical, emotional (intrinsically), and mental well-being. Sleep, a healthy diet, and good cleanliness are only a small part of self-care. It also entails being highly aware of your glorious body and your ever-wondering mind and attending to their demands. Self-care improves your focus, output, and productivity while assisting in the maintenance of a positive partner relationship.

SIGNS YOUR RELATIONSHIP MAY NEED SELF-CARE

There are indicators that you might need to exercise self-care in your relationship that can guide you in the right direction.

- Feeling overly burdened by your partner's expectations of you.
- Doubting that you'll ever have the energy or time to do what must be done.
- Feeling angry about your partner's time to themselves.
- Feeling as though you're unsure of what you want or what you're lacking

IMPORTANCE OF SELF-CARE IN MAINTAINING HEALTHY RELATIONSHIPS

Self-care helps to lessen codependency. Taking care of oneself enables you to recognize and cherish your worth as a person. This means that feeling good about yourself does not require constant validation from your partner.

For instance, while reading a good book might increase your knowledge, certain gym exercises can help you rock an amazing figure. This increases your confidence, self-love, and self-esteem. It becomes easier to love and esteem yourself as a person when you are able to share that love with your other half.

It makes your sexual life better.

You will understand your body's requirements on all levels when you devote more time to taking care of it. Once you realize what makes you happy, what your sexual preferences are, you'll want to share them with your partner. Place value on your own physical needs while also taking into account your partner's needs, determine what pleases you both, and once you reach a shared understanding, this will make your sexual life better.

By exercising self-care, you show your partner how to treat you.

Instead of telling your partner how you want to be loved, it is easier to show them. More often than not, they will copy your actions if they observe you making an effort to look after yourself the best you can. This opens up additional channels for your partner to understand your needs, goals, and constraints.

Self-care immediately becomes important to a partner who loves and values you when it is important to you.

It improves both you as a person and a lover.

Your physique and the way you interact with others and your partner both show how emotionally, physically, and psychologically spent you are. You cannot pour from an empty cup; therefore, if you feel depressed, unmotivated, or angry, it's likely that you are not taking good care of yourself.

As a result, you will need to spend some time caring for yourself in order to care for others. It would appear that in order to spread love to others, you must first cultivate a deep love for yourself.

THE BENEFITS OF SELF-CARE FOR RELATIONSHIPS

1. More presence

You will have more room for one another if you practice self-care in your relationship when you and your partner do get together.

Being present is essential for maintaining a connection in a long-term, committed relationship like marriage. It's not about physically being there; rather, it's about mentally being present and prepared to participate, which is difficult to accomplish when you're stressed out and overburdened with everything else on your plate in life.

This isn't about the busyness of life either; it's about

being able to show up with your partner focused on them, not half listening to them while the other half of your brain tries to solve that problem at work and simultaneously tries to remember what the heck you needed to grab at the store but didn't. By taking care of yourself, you'll be more prepared to interact with your partner in a deliberate, present manner. We should expect more from one another than just the bare minimum, don't you think?

2. Less reactive

This is a crucial one. In a relationship, it's quite easy to default to reaction mode—trust me, I know this well! Reactivity is when we respond to a "trigger" from a place of often high emotional pain and/or pre-programmed response because we lack the time, headspace, or emotional maturity to do so wisely. Unsurprisingly, this typically does not result in improved communication.

If we exercise self-care, we are more likely to be in a better mental state where we can truly hear what our partner is saying without all the pre-programmed automatic answers racing to the fore of our minds, ready to explode out of our mouths and scorching the ground around us. Improved self-care results in improved communication.

3. A deeper connection

When you think of how self-care might benefit your relationship, this may not be the first benefit that comes to mind, but the reality is that intimacy—both physical and emotional—is difficult to maintain when a person is under a lot of stress and pressure. Do you recall the last time you struggled to find time for a healthy dinner, a restful night's sleep, or even a long enough shower because you had way too much on your plate? That doesn't promote emotional or psychological intimacy, right?

The idea behind how self-care and relationships interact is that when we show up with our partner in a way that can honor their needs, we are taking care of ourselves and genuinely and honestly honoring our needs.

4. Stronger boundaries

Boundaries may seem like a wall set up to prevent someone from interacting with us in a particular way for those of us who grew up with little limits, but they are actually more like guidelines or paint on the roads intended to prevent us from veering off in the wrong direction. You are assisting your partner in staying out of the ditch of your expectations when you establish clear boundaries with them around things like time, money, and even intimacy and communication demands!

A boundary-less person, for instance, might never inform their partner that their expectation of physical closeness every night is more than they want or can handle. Eventually, this causes resentment and may even result in an argument during which harmful words are said. Or perhaps your partner's spending habits are stressing you out by depleting the household budget. Someone is going to end up careening off the road if you can't come to a consensus on what the expectations will be surrounding that thing, and you can't be honest about what your wants and needs are. Setting boundaries is essential for self-care and a healthy relationship.

SELF-CARE VS. SELF-LOVE: LOVING YOURSELF IN A RELATIONSHIP

You and your partner must both be in good health for your relationship to be successful. Physical health is crucial at all times, but it isn't exactly what we mean here, rather that your ability to support and care for your own mental and emotional well-being must come from both you and your partner. Regardless of how much you and your partner may love one another, you cannot put off taking care of yourself. Regardless of the stage your relationship is in; it can be very easy to lose yourself in it. Nevertheless, it's important to maintain a connection with yourself so that you can assess your mental and emotional health and take steps to improve it. This is often easier said than done; however, focusing on two different ideas, self-care and self-love, can help you keep in touch with yourself in order to be more present for your relationship, your partner, and yourself.

Although the terms self-care and self-love sound similar and are sometimes confused, they are actually quite different, and both are crucial to monitor and seek out when you're in a relationship. While self-love is being kind to oneself, self-care refers to looking after one's physical and emotional well-being. Being able to care for and love yourself will enable you to be more caring and present with your partner, which can help build the bonds between you two. If the concepts of self-care and self-love seem a little abstract to you, here are a few ways you can put them into practice in your daily life.

WAYS TO PRACTICE SELF-CARE IN A RELATIONSHIP

1. Planning alone time

Maintaining your sense of self is crucial whether you are just starting a relationship or have been with your partner since time immemorial. Preserving your sense of self means that you should acknowledge and stay in-tune with your wants and well-being even when you are in a relationship. Finding or making time for alone reflection allows you to take a fresh breath, check in with yourself, and assess your emotional state.

Whether you're an introvert or an extrovert, it's crucial to schedule some alone time occasionally so you can check in with yourself. This kind of event may need to happen daily for some people, but it may just occur sometimes for others. You know yourself best, so frequency and duration are irrelevant as long as you are consciously choosing to be alone and check-in. To spend time apart from your partner in order to have a healthier connection may sound contradictory, but hear me out! Without being in excellent health yourself, you cannot be a decent partner.

In relationships where you truly love the other person, it can be quite challenging for many people to prioritize their needs. But in order for you to be the best version of yourself, this is essential. You will be a better friend, partner, support system, and all of the other crucial responsibilities in a relationship after you take care of your personal needs. Sometimes spending some alone time identifying your needs is the only way to take care of them. Self-care in a relationship depends on staying aware of your needs and knowing how to meet them.

2. Establishing boundaries

Establishing boundaries is a crucial component of any relationship, as you know we've already covered in-depth in

Chapter 4. It's worth mentioning again that it's necessary to spend some time alone, even when you're in a relationship. Establishing boundaries can help you take the time, space, and even the required distance (if needed) to take care of your mental, physical, and emotional well-being.

Together with these kinds of boundaries, it's crucial to talk to your partner about your physical and even digital boundaries so that you are both on the same page and that your needs are being met. Do you feel at ease with PDA (public display of affection)? Do you anticipate a prompt text reply from your partner? Or if they don't pick up, to call you back right away? Or is it expected that your partner won't frequently blow up your phone?

You can make sure that you are honoring each other's wants and allowing each other to feel supported in the relationship by communicating these expectations and boundaries often and explicitly. Even though it might feel awkward at first, communicating your needs is an essential component of any form of self-care. By being honest about your boundaries, expectations, and wishes, you can enable your partner to help you as much as they can.

It should go without saying, but it's also critical to pay attention to and respect your partner's boundaries when they express them to you. Another crucial component of a successful relationship is giving your partner time and space to take care of themselves.

3. Controlling stress level

Under stress, no one is at their best. There are countless ways that stress can appear, but most of the time, it does so adversely and has a big impact on your interpersonal relationship. If you're like me, you might have a tendency to lose it when you're extremely stressed out, snapping at anyone who gets in your way without apparent cause. Sadly, because we trust them and are typically close by, it's all too easy to vent on our loved ones. It's never right to vent your frustration on someone else, especially not your partner, no matter how stressed you are.

Avoiding the stressful scenario entirely is an excellent method to reduce this because it might be difficult to maintain total control in stressful situations. While it is not feasible to completely free yourself from stress, it is possible to lower your stress levels, which can help you deal with stressful situations more effectively. You can minimize stress in your life by doing things like getting adequate sleep, being better at time management, and learning how to set good boundaries. Yet, some forms of stress can't be avoided, so you just have to learn how to manage them.

Exercise, yoga, meditation, and pastimes like baking, painting, or general artistic endeavors are all excellent coping mechanisms. Mostly anything that allows you to unwind, relax and focus on something other than the things you cannot control. It might take a lot of effort and commitment to successfully manage your stress by eliminating needless stress and/or developing coping mechanisms. Although stress management can be challenging, doing so will have a hugely good impact on your relationships and personal life!

WAYS TO PRACTICE SELF-LOVE IN A RELATIONSHIP

1. Being present

Being told to "be present" can seem rather impersonal; after all, you are present because you are here, right?

WRONG! Being present is much more than just being in the physical state. Being present entails being aware of your feelings, paying attention to your surroundings, and choosing your words and actions carefully. It can be easy to put life on autopilot and coast through it, but this attitude does not support self-love or fulfilling relationships.

It's crucial to express all of your feelings, both positive and negative, in order to deal with them and move on in a better and healthier way. Mindfulness training is a helpful method to be present. A very easy form of meditation called mindfulness can help you in being more introspective, relaxed, and centered. There are a ton of mindfulness resources available, including books, apps, and guided meditations that can assist you in connecting with yourself and practicing presence. Using positive affirmations and intention-setting techniques is another method to remain present. For those who enjoy lists and organizations, this tactic may work well.

Create a list of the goals you want to achieve, such as noticing both happy and bad emotions as they occur, talking to yourself positively, setting boundaries with others, and focusing on the positive aspects of yourself. You'll feel happier and more confident when you're present and nice to yourself, which will enable you to give your relationship and yourself your best.

2. Becoming aware of your emotions

This was briefly discussed when we talked about being present in your relationship and for yourself, but it's important to delve a little deeper into this idea. Understanding your emotions is a crucial component of loving yourself. You need to check in with yourself and give yourself room to consider your feelings and mood. Recognizing your emotions is vital, but it's not the main goal.

It's crucial to acknowledge your feelings and take them as they are. Many people have the attitude of "why can't I be more laid back" or "I shouldn't be upset; people have it much worse than me" when they react to anything. However, this kind of evaluation is unhealthy because it invalidates and ignores very real emotions. First of all, congratulate yourself on your progress if you start to notice negative thought patterns because it shows you are reflecting deeply. Not everyone has the self-awareness necessary to recognize these types of ingrained habits. Following this, it's crucial to treat oneself kindly and without passing judgment on these emotions. Instead, strive to reinterpret your thought patterns or point of view into a positive and self-affirming lens that boosts you up.

Because you are eliminating criticism and negative self-talk, accepting your feelings will help you feel greater love for yourself. You will be able to treat yourself and your partner with more compassion if you are in touch with your emotions, deal with them, and express them. This type of self-love promotion will enhance both your personal and romantic relationships.

3. Trying to establish spiritual ties

Self-love is often both a personal and a spiritual journey for many people. Many popular self-love practices, including mindfulness, yoga, meditation, and prayer, have their roots in spirituality and organized religion. A greater purpose can be provided for your practices by engaging in meditation and prayer in a spiritual or religious context.

In addition to these methods, it may be beneficial to look

for religious gatherings where you feel comfortable worshipping, such as a church, synagogue, or temple. In addition to making you more grounded and deliberate, seeking a spiritual or religious connection can also help you in embracing self-love.

Whatever faith you practice, acceptance and love are universal themes. You can try bringing self-love into your weekly routine by engaging with these ideas on a regular basis (such as at your Sunday church). Even if you are not religious, using religious or spiritual readings to help you with your introspection while engaging in self-love routines and rituals can be beneficial. This is not to argue that adding spirituality is the only method to practice self-love; rather, it is to state that this is often beneficial for those who find it challenging to carve out enough time for themselves.

Because it becomes a part of your religious or spiritual practice, seeking a spiritual connection can also assist you in maintaining a self-love routine. The pursuit of spirituality and religion can help you on your path to self-love, which can enhance your relationship regardless of your partner's beliefs. These pursuits, however, are very personal and are not necessarily things you need to discuss with your partner. The pursuit of self-love through this kind of practice can also be extremely wonderful if you and your partner have similar religious or spiritual convictions.

ADOPTING SELF-CARE HABITS IN A RELATIONSHIP

Sometimes the upheavals and modifications in our life are desperately needed. Perhaps forming a "we" has given you the confidence to start believing in other people. Perhaps becoming a "we" has motivated you to sharpen your focus so you can finally go after your aspirations.

So, what if you've been experiencing some odd feelings? If you've asked yourself, "Who am I now that I am a "we"? What do you do? What if you're beginning to recognize that you're losing other desirable aspects of yourself?

It's time to take action if you've noticed that you're not quite the same person you previously were and you're unhappy about it:

Avoid blaming

When you're feeling a little lost or trapped in life to look around, it's easy to want to blame what's right in front of you. If you find yourself staring at your partner and growing angrier by the second because you believe it is their fault you aren't feeling like yourself, take a deep breath and realize that this is your problem to solve.

Investigate

For each person, losing oneself takes a different form. You must try to increase your awareness of what you sense might be missing from your life. Remember to recall a point in your life when you were particularly confident. You were at ease with yourself and exuded self-assurance. Your truest and finest selves are here.

It could have been a brief period or a significant portion of your life. Imagine yourself in that situation while closing your eyes. Where were you? What were you doing? Were you alone or with another person? Once you have a mental description of the scene, write it down. What were you pondering, feeling, or going through? These are crucial hints for solving the "who am I" riddle.

Find your passions again

Look at the notes you made when you were most your truest self. You must have regularly engaged in activities that made you feel like yourself. What were those concepts or convictions that you were so passionate about? How did you act upon such notions or convictions?

You want to identify the regular activities that gave you confidence. Perhaps such passions were truly interests or hobbies. Perhaps those passions had nothing to do with hobbies but rather with your job, family, a cause close to your heart, or an organization you belonged to.

It's time to return to "it," whatever that may be for you.

Recommit to friendship

Everyone has known a friend who unexpectedly fell in love and vanished. And after we started dating someone new, we all started playing the "I'm going to hang with him or her tonight" card whenever our friends called on a Saturday night. Unfortunately, when we fall in love, our friends suffer the most.

Once you're in a relationship, spending every evening with your spouse or partner is easy. It's time to put money back into your friendships; this time, it needs to last.

* * *

Self-care is an essential aspect of building and maintaining healthy relationships. When you take care of yourself emotionally, physically, and mentally, it not only benefits you as an individual but also strengthens your connection with your partner and others. By prioritizing your needs and setting boundaries, you are better equipped to communicate effectively, handle conflict positively, and build a foundation of trust and respect in your relationship. Remember, self-care is not selfish but rather an essential component of a fulfilling and sustainable partnership. By investing in yourself, you are investing in the health and longevity of your relationship.

MAKE A CONSCIOUS EFFORT TO CHOOSE LOVE AND CONNECTION

"Love is a choice you make from moment to moment." — *Barbara De Angelis*

RIGHT AT THE START OF THE BOOK, we talked about the story of Alexis and Jeremy, which serves as a potent reminder of the value of prioritizing our relationships and the five key elements of a healthy relationship. Because of their and others' stories, plus my own experiences – that is how I came to the realization that a loving relationship is a continuous choice and effort to make it work... and being able to share guidance with those who desire success in their relationship was the driving force behind writing this book.

In order to have a long-lasting relationship, we can learn from the faults of our past... and if we really want to succeed, we can learn, too, from the trials others have overcome.

But faults and failures aren't our only guiding force. We learn through reading, through watching, through observing, through sharing our experiences... and this is where you as the reader have a chance to be part of the guiding process and inspiration for others who desire to attain a lifelong loving relationship.

As relationship expert De Angelis' quote above suggests, love is a continuous choice that we make in each moment of our relationships. Therefore, to maintain a healthy relationship, we need to be open to learning and growing together, and choose love and connection over fear and separation.

You may not have the expertise or career experience of

psychologists and relationship experts, but you do have an opportunity to contribute to helping other people find their path to attaining a long-lasting relationship with their partner that many dream of.

By leaving a review of this book on Amazon and/or Goodreads, you'll show other people who want to be in a happy, fulfilling, healthy, loving relationship where they can find the guidance they're looking for.

By the simple act of telling other readers how this book helped you and what they can expect to find inside, you'll help start their discovery and their own roadmap to a loving partnership that will last a lifetime.

Thank you for your support. There may be more work ahead of you in your relationship journey, but whatever direction you're heading in, this is a great start. Sharing our learnings and experiences helps encourage other people and inspires them to take the next steps forward in their own relationships.

Now that we've covered the 5 keys to building lifelong healthy relationships, let's delve into the next part of this book where we will explore further steps to enhance your love and connection.

SCAN THE QR CODE TO LEAVE A REVIEW

PART II

CHAPTER 7: BUILDING A DEEPER CONNECTION

*I*t's easy to lose that special connection that makes you feel at ease with your sweetheart as you go about your regular activities, day after day, month after month. You will notice that you are growing emotionally distant from your lover if you haven't been spending enough time with them recently, and that is not a good sensation. "Us time" is just as important as the desire for "me time," if not more so.

There are various ways to strengthen your relationship with your partner and involve them in your learning path. One of them is engaging in a shared pastime or trying something new. Also, set aside some time each day to express and talk about your emotions and worries. Take the opportunity to clear up any misunderstandings you believe are keeping you from bonding with one another.

All of us desire stronger bonds with the people we care about. Sadly, sometimes achieving what we want can be very difficult since it takes time and effort to build these deep, long-lasting, healthy relationships.

You need to set the foundation for these deep connections with your partner. When it comes to romance, you can end yourself swimming in the shallow end if you don't have the right attitude, approach, and instruction.

PRACTICING VULNERABILITY IN YOUR RELATIONSHIP

Being vulnerable is one of the most crucial steps in developing a strong bond with your partner. Being open and honest about your emotions in a relationship entails saying "I love you" out loud. Being vulnerable in a relationship entails expressing our feelings while not knowing how the other person would react.

Being vulnerable implies being open to differences with others or even rejection. Because of this, vulnerability—despite sounding easy—is significantly more difficult to achieve.

Being open to the possibility of unfavorable outcomes and taking a risk, even when you have no control over the outcome, are at the heart of vulnerability in relationships.

Vulnerability in relationships fosters closeness and connection and is essential to building strong, long-lasting bonds despite the inherent danger.

How can you be more vulnerable with your partner?

There are stages to help you on this road if you're unsure of how to start becoming more vulnerable in relationships.

1. Take things easy.

Instead of starting with what you cannot do, do what you

can. Although it seems straightforward, we all make the mistake of focusing on a goal for which we are not yet prepared.

Start being vulnerable more often if you want to be able to open up more. First, practice relationship vulnerability inside your comfort zone. Then, iterate continually and get better every day.

Your comfort zone will gradually grow, and you will finally be able to do things that were previously impossible for you.

2. Recognize the necessity for emotional boundaries.

When we are young, we learn by watching. Although it used to be true, we no longer need to shield ourselves. What were the main lessons you learned about being honest when you were a kid and a young adult? Why do you think it's important to protect your vulnerability in relationships?

Understanding the source of your vulnerability fears might help you overcome them.

3. Go slowly and pay attention

You may be prone to losing sight of how you truly feel if you have a tendency to suppress or avoid expressing your emotions.

Focus on the here and now and ask yourself why you are feeling and thinking the way you are. If you want to better understand your emotional life, keep a journal, practice meditation, or go to counseling.

4. Share your difficulties

Talk to your partner about your issues with vulnerability in relationships while you work on being more open. Their tolerance and empathy for you will grow as a result.

Go ahead and share, even if all you can say at the time is that you don't share readily. They will be able to see a small portion of your inner world through this window.

5. Be more vocal about your needs and emotions

Be truthful when expressing your ideas, desires, and feelings. Every time, give a little more. Locate the boundary where you feel exposed but not too far out of your comfort zone.

Practice being vulnerable every day by speaking your true feelings.

It's likely that you may recall a time when someone confided in you and how compassionate you were in your response. A vulnerable gesture elicits a compassionate response from others.

Keep that in mind when you begin to worry or fear rejection.

6. Ask for help

You can get more support the more you ask for it. And this will encourage you to inquire and divulge more.

Also, it becomes easier to develop intimacy and discuss fears and doubts with your loved one.

If you are having trouble, there is also professional assistance available. You can start to open up more and find the source of your worries with the assistance of a psychologist in order to reach higher levels of closeness.

BE OPEN TO BEING VULNERABLE IN RELATIONSHIPS.

Vulnerability in relationships is significant because of how it affects our relationships. In a relationship, being vulnerable fosters greater closeness, self-love, and feelings of worth and recognition.

Only if we are prepared to take the risk of being open and vulnerable can we feel a sense of profound connection and closeness.

Many of us have strong, frequently unconscious phobias about being vulnerable in relationships. You don't need to be an expert if you're unsure about how to communicate vulnerability. Just proceed incrementally.

Be fair to yourself and honest with your partner about your challenges because nobody becomes better at something overnight. With the people you care about, push yourself to have the bravery to share a little bit more of yourself each day. This openness will enhance your bonds.

BEING PRESENT IN A RELATIONSHIP

It takes presence to learn how to be in a relationship healthily. Being present entails being conscious of how you are interacting with others.

That corresponds to the amount of focus you offer that person. Being present essentially means that you are conscious of giving a loved one your undivided, unconditional love.

Passing judgment or expressing an ego is not allowed when one is present at the moment. No distractions or agendas. The goal is to just experience a "soul-to-soul" connection with the other person right now.

It should be fairly easy and straightforward to understand. You are "offering" someone with energy, a connection, your time, and attention while being completely receptive to what they have to say.

WHY IS BEING PRESENT IN A RELATIONSHIP IMPORTANT?

Being present in relationships is crucial for a successful relationship. An authentic connection is created when two people make a conscious, cooperative effort to enjoy being by themselves with one another without disruptions, interruptions, or interference and without allowing moments from the past or something in the future to threaten what you currently have.

You must first be aware of yourself in order to enjoy such a rewarding experience. The ability to participate at the moment, with what is happening right now, with genuine delight and passion free of doubt, regrets, concern, or even fear, can take some time to develop.

When you apply it to your connections, it enables you to concentrate on the ones that are significant to you, especially your partner.

While you are dealing with this individual, all the other chaos and daily obligations are put on hold. Also, your loved one will be able to sense your presence and will reciprocate with the same energy.

10 TIPS ON HOW TO BE PRESENT IN A RELATIONSHIP

It's essential to establish a connection with oneself prior to being present in a relationship.

Without being conscious of your actions, it might be difficult to be entirely aware of your level of interaction with another individual. Partners, in particular, can work on being more present by:

1. Self-care routine

You must make sure to practice regular self-care. You can consciously focus on someone else in this way. Journaling is a great way to evaluate oneself.

Once you've finished writing, go back to the entry from the day before to get a better picture of where you could be falling short and how to become more present in a relationship.

2. Create a space for mindfulness and meditation

Many techniques of mindfulness or meditation can be used, but they all aim to bring you into the present moment.

It will be easier for you to give someone else your entire, undivided attention once you become cognizant of this area.

3. Establish parameters for the relationship.

Being present in a relationship is the cornerstone of a healthy circumstance, whether one is married or just dating. Setting limits that designate intentional time spent together is one way to do that.

That entails shutting off connectivity; no use of the internet, social media, or business at particular times when the two of you should be able to interact without interruption.

Meal times, the end of the day, possibly dating nights, and weekend getaways should all be included on your list. They are perfect for connecting without outside distractions.

4. Texting is acceptable

Sending encouraging texts throughout the day with open-ended questions or topics that pique the other person's interest might encourage active listening and conversation when the phones are put away at night when you're apart from one another. Be mindful not to overdo the frequency though to the point that it causes a distraction or smothers the other person.

Because you have to be careful about the stuff you send, this acts as a kind of virtual presence that gets the other person ready for an evening of "presence."

5. Wear the appropriate attire.

Spending time with the people you love doesn't always need you to be dressed to the nines.

Sometimes, having a meaningful conversation while relaxing on the couch in a t-shirt and sweating and drinking hot cocoa is soothing.

I did refer to hot cocoa. You should avoid using alcohol, even wine if you wish to listen attentively and give someone your complete, lucid attention.

However, if we're in a long-term relationship, we don't always give enough care to how we dress, how we style our hair, or how we look in general.

This is an additional effort to be mindful of love and to dress appropriately for those times when spending time with your partner is more important than using technology.

6. Share secrets with each other

Make sure your partner is the first person you confide

information to, including reactions to things, updates on significant life events, opinions, and private information.

By doing this, you're actively trying to be there for your partner by forging a stronger bond.

7. Arrange a time to exchange critiques.

If you and your partner have similar tastes in music, novels, art, or movies, start a couple's book club or swap playlists, and then spend an evening discussing what you both learned from the experience.

That could result in an evening of insightful conversation as well as the possibility of each of you discovering new hobbies, interests, and opportunities for outings.

You may also check out art exhibits, concerts, and book signings for your favorite authors.

8. Remember to listen

Many people are chronic overachievers, which makes it necessary to learn how to be present in a relationship.

One issue is that some people make an effort to focus on the present moment with someone by asking questions, but they fail to grasp that active listening is a skill that requires practice as well.

When someone is expressing themselves, they need to be energetically supported and paid attention to.

People don't like to look at a face that is expressionless, or that appears to be impatiently anticipating a new question.

9. Show up

Being present in a relationship entails turning up on time

as promised. Being late or, worse yet, failing to show up for whatever reason without calling is rude to a relationship.

If you repeatedly show up at the last minute, the other person can start to think they don't matter or that you don't want to be there.

Pay attention to how you present yourself; you don't want to make an incorrect impression.

10. Express gratitude to one another

If you've been in a relationship for any length of time, gratitude is often only understood and never expressed. Making gratitude an expressed priority rather than a quiet nod is vital for those who are making a conscious effort to be present in a relationship.

You will begin to achieve presence when each of you is consciously aware of the other's appreciation for even the smallest effort, being who each of you is as people with remarkable traits.

EXHIBITING MORE CURIOSITY IN YOUR RELATIONSHIP WITH YOUR PARTNER

Perhaps the first things that come to mind when you consider the essential elements of a relationship are communication, dispute resolution, physical intimacy, etc. Curiosity is one thing that is often forgotten but ought to be at the top of that list.

Curiosity is one of the cornerstones of a solid relationship, according to decades of research by the Gottman Institute. The other concepts mentioned in this research are healing and reuniting after disagreements and navigating conflicts in beneficial ways.

In this context, being curious means showing interest in your partner's life and experiences. The relationship may deteriorate if time passes and we don't check in with our partners to see how they're doing on a regular basis.

One method to prevent becoming two coexisting humans with our partners is to maintain a sense of curiosity.

SEVEN TECHNIQUES TO INCREASE CURIOSITY IN YOUR RELATIONSHIP

You can express interest in your relationship in a variety of ways. Here are some pointers:

- Ask your partner about their day. Asking questions is a terrific approach to demonstrating interest.
- Ask questions that are specific. It's okay to ask how things went at work, but it's better to ask how that morning meeting went.
- Ask open-ended questions. Ask questions that begin with something like "Tell me about..." "How do you feel about..." and "Why do you believe..." to avoid "yes" or "no" questions.
- Lean in to find out more. Using what they have said as a basis, ask follow-up questions.
- Be active and physically present. Avoid being distracted by other things, such as your phone, and maintain eye contact during the talk.
- Use active listening techniques. Ask if you understand correctly by rephrasing and repeating back some of the information they provide (for example, "It sounds like your meeting this morning was intense yet productive. Is that right?").

- Engage in conversations that go beyond the ordinary. What they're looking forward to, how they feel about their friendships, any great moments they want to remember, etc.

USING WORDS OF AFFIRMATION IN YOUR RELATIONSHIP

Another strategy for creating a strong connection with your partner is to use words of affirmation. Actions always speak louder than words - Unless, of course, "words of affirmation" is your partner's love language. In this situation, words are crucial. A person whose major love language is words of affirmation will value what you have to say to them highly, whether it is spoken or written.

Even when you want them to just let things go, the words you choose will have a big impact on them. In fact, it's not unusual for short sentences like "I'm grateful for..." and "I love how you..." to go a great way toward expressing how much someone is valued.

Compliments, heartfelt gratitude, handwritten letters, and learning what they mean to other people are all things that your partner will particularly appreciate. The goal is to express to your lover how much you value and care about them.

EXAMPLES OF WORDS OF AFFIRMATION

A few examples of words of affirmation include the following:

- "When you're here, everything is better."
- "I appreciate you taking the time to..."

- "I couldn't do this without you."
- "The new attire is absolutely beautiful. You look fantastic in it!"
- "I feel very fortunate to be with you."
- "Thank you very much for being in my life."
- "I was impressed when you..."
- "I appreciate you..."
- "You are working so hard, and it shows. I'm incredibly happy for you."
- "One of my favorite persons to be with is you."
- "You mean the world to me."
- "You are the very best"
- "Your help meant the world to me."
- "You're a model for me!"

USING WORDS OF AFFIRMATION: SOME TIPS

One whose main love language is words of affirmation might be moved by finding a beautiful note on the kitchen counter, a post-it note in the center of the mirror, or a favorite poem lyric stashed away in a suitcase, to name just a few of the numerous possibilities.

If words of affirmation are your partner's main form of expression, you must discover effective ways to tell them you cherish them. Here are some pointers on how to communicate with your lover in their love language.

Don't fake it

If you want to connect with someone who uses words of affirmation as their major love language, be sure to be genuine in your communication. They will be able to detect if you are making things up, so you want to make sure that whatever you say to them is genuine.

Be compassionate

It's important for your partner to know that you understand how they're feeling when it comes to words of affirmation, especially if they're feeling low. Be sympathetic to your partner. Consider what it would be like to walk in their shoes and then indicate that you realize how they are feeling.

Express your gratitude

Those that flourish when others acknowledge and appreciate what they do are typically those who find fulfillment in kind words and compliments. The trick is to express your gratitude to them clearly, whether it is for the way they wash the laundry, the dinner they made, or the three hours they spent proofreading your report.

It will make their heart smile and fill their tank if you are clear about what you really enjoyed. So, don't be reluctant.

Plenty of "I love yous."

Even though it may seem overused at times, the recipient of your words of affirmation won't be weary of hearing them, especially if you discover fresh and original ways to express your affection.

Send a letter to them

When you're in a rush, email is a terrific way to communicate, but there's something unique about getting a love letter in the mail. Now take a pencil and piece of paper and begin writing. When your partner receives the letter, he or she will be completely taken aback. If writing them, a letter sounds daunting, get them a cute card and include a kind remark inside.

Put up a note

Using a sticky note to leave your partner a brief message about how much they mean to you can sometimes be the greatest and most effective way to express your love for them. If you're feeling very imaginative, you could scrawl several notes in the shape of a heart or another object on their car's window or their bathroom mirror.

Send them a shout out

Make sure to praise your partner for words of affirmation in public. Tell them your proudest accomplishments and the things you value most. Telling others how amazing you believe your partner is will impact their hearts in a variety of ways, but don't go overboard and humiliate your relationship. Hence, be generous with your praise. This is a wonderful approach to making your lover feel more loved.

Proclaim their virtues

When your partner is depressed or disheartened, it's crucial to highlight their positive qualities. Giving them a pep talk and highlighting the qualities or activities they excel at says a lot. They must understand that you value who they are.

Dial it up

Increase your use of kind words while your partner is going through a difficult time. Be especially nice and compassionate while reassuring your lover of their value and your appreciation for them. It is always beneficial to provide words of encouragement. These actions demonstrate to them that you are there for them through good times and bad.

HOW TO DEVELOP A WORDS OF AFFIRMATION HABIT

Even if you are not a proponent of affirmations, it is a good idea to incorporate them into your daily routine. Even if it might not come naturally, there are steps you can take to develop the practice of giving words of affirmation:

- Try using your partner's pet name as the first word in every conversation. You can say, for example, "Good morning, gorgeous," or "How are you, sweetheart?" These compliments may come off as corny, but to someone who values words of affirmation, they might mean something special.
- Be yourself: Avoid putting too much pressure on yourself or expressing untrue feelings. Just allow yourself to be who you truly are and express your admiration for your lover.
- Encourage your partner: Affirmations don't simply have to be thanks or praises; they can also be phrases that boost your partner's confidence. Tell them you believe in them and support them when they show interest in something or share one of their ambitions with you.

CHAPTER 8: KEEPING THE ROMANCE ALIVE IN LONG-TERM RELATIONSHIPS

*H*ow to keep the spark alive in marriages and committed relationships is one of the hardest challenges you may have.

Throughout many years and millennia, people have fought to keep the spark alive in committed relationships. So how can long-term relationships rekindle their spark?

Extensive descriptions of love, passion, and romance that seem to be reserved for the young and new relationships abound in literature. For years, writers and poets have lamented how difficult it is to remember and record this experience.

Marriage and other long-term relationships have historically characterized the family and social structure. Even if many Western cultures have opened up to alternative types of relationships, millions of people still seek out stability and long-term relationships.

The sexual spark is often elusive and difficult to maintain, even in the most secure and enduring relationships, which causes interpersonal discomfort, conflict, resentment, and boredom. This raises the issue of why people seek long-term relationships.

WHY DO PEOPLE CHOOSE LONG-TERM RELATIONSHIPS?

The desire for long-term ties and relationships can be understood in a variety of ways. Evolutionary, survival, existential, and purpose are a few of them.

Humans are sociable creatures who want human contact. Most people connect with others through their families, friends, and communities, and many facets of our lives are set up to support this.

Several studies have shown how being disconnected from others and being isolated from society have catastrophic and negative repercussions. Long-term relationships can provide a level of dedication that ensures a solid bond throughout the course of a lifetime.

In the past, people formed committed relationships to ensure their survival. Families formed ties in order to do business, secure lands for tribes, and establish paternity. Children were employed in farming, helping one another and guaranteeing survival.

Any arrangement other than marriage meant definite hardship or death for women, who could not generally survive without a husband or father.

The societal view of marriage was shaped in part by this reality. However, long-term relationships have other advantages outside the need for survival. Humans have emotional demands for belonging, connection, and being seen and heard. These demands may have evolved to foster a closer bond and assure survival.

Regardless of the evolutionary origin, people have the

aforementioned emotional demands. Even if many people nowadays may live happily alone or in short-term relationships, people still look for and enter into them.

This is mostly motivated by the emotional urge for a secure relationship. Long-term relationships, in their optimum state, offer this emotional connection. To develop this kind of relationship, many people put in years of effort.

WHY DOES THE INITIAL SPARK IN LONG-TERM RELATIONSHIPS FADE AWAY?

We must understand what sparks the light in the first place in order to understand why it fades. The first spark that people experience in relationships is mostly caused by a combination of novelty and simplicity, both of which are transient elements.

Novelty is something that is fresh and a little strange, whether it is a person, item, or event. Novelty causes the brain to release large amounts of dopamine, making people feel happy.

Dopamine levels rise in personal relationships as a result of new partners and different types of sexual activity, producing strong emotions that might occasionally border on intoxication and euphoria. The opposite of novelty is regularity and familiarity, which over time, causes dopamine levels to drop.

In addition to being novel, a relationship's beginning is comparatively straightforward in comparison to the practical and emotional complexity that emerges with time. Many couples do not live together or share substantial responsibilities at the start of their relationships. They often spend just enough time together to feel terrific with separate living quarters to retreat to when necessary. Also, dopamine-fueled emotions enable the mind to exalt a partner and ignore problems. Everything in this adds to the "spark." A few causes for the fading of the spark in long-term relationships are the following:

1. The spark is merely transient

The early spark of a relationship diminishes as the novelty wears off, and attention turns toward connection and attachment as the relationship deepens. Dopamine levels drop with familiarity, and other brain chemicals take over in the bonding process.

The feeling of a sexual spark may lessen as a result of this change. Understanding that this process is typical and predictable is crucial. It then becomes a matter of determining whether a spark can be rekindled in a secure relationship or if something fresh and innovative is required.

2. Secure connection and excitement

Relationship and sex therapy professionals disagree on what causes and sustains sexual chemistry in a relationship. Relationship specialists contend that stronger bond results in more fulfilling sexual interactions and can promote a more mature sexual spark.

According to sex therapy experts, intimacy and familiarity stifle sexual enthusiasm, while novelty and a little healthy distance might foster or sustain it.

3. Responsive versus spontaneous desire

The predominance of responsive desire is another characteristic of long-term relationships. It's common to experience intense, spontaneous desire or libido that seems to fuel itself at the beginning of a new relationship.

Over time, spontaneous desire often transforms into a responsive desire.

This implies that people can respond to a partner's approaches and other stimuli in addition to merely feeling like they are in the mood.

Many people and couples question where the spark vanished and how to rekindle it as a result of this shift, which is often ignored or improperly handled. Sexual excitement can be created and maintained with the right knowledge and management of responsive desire in a long-term, committed relationship.

4. Sexual spark needs efforts

Whether it is closeness or distance, it takes effort to recover and keep the sexual spark in a long-term relationship. Striving for a spark is not an indication of pathology in a person or a relationship. It should be seen as a chance to collaborate with a partner and develop a relationship process.

Too many people give up or decide to quit a relationship because they believe that the presence of a sexual spark indicates that it is healthy. Strangely, the absence of a spark could indicate a strong, mature connection that needs to strive to keep things exciting.

5. Sexual dysfunction

Sexual dysfunction can happen for one partner or both as higher levels of arousal fade. In long-term relationships, problems, including erectile dysfunction, delayed ejaculation, sexual pain, and desire concerns, are becoming more prevalent.

Sexual excitement is a vital element of healthy and vigorous sexual function. The orgasm process and blood flow to the genitals are both significantly influenced by the brain. Excitation is often what triggers this process.

Sexual excitement and sexual function are more likely to be inhibited if there isn't a spark between you and your partner.

10 STRATEGIES FOR PRESERVING A RELATIONSHIP'S SPARK

How do we maintain the spark? These are a few easy and doable strategies for reigniting the flame in committed relationships.

1. Request a different thing each week.

Understanding what "the spark" means to you is the first step in keeping it alive. Given that we all have different love languages, it is likely that what makes you and your partner feel loved and valued is different. This implies that we also express our love in a variety of ways. Trust your relationship enough to ask for what you want rather than hoping your partner would love you in the way you desire or be resentful when they don't.

Try to turn it into a game by deciding on a very specific task for each of you to complete during each week before it begins. Perhaps you want them to arrange a surprise date, bring you flowers one day, or say something kind about your appearance. Perhaps they'll want more one-on-one time with you or more flattering comments about their job. Even if it's only meant to last a week, actions will teach your partner how to make you feel loved in addition to the things that do. If they notice how pleased it makes you when they really do it, they'll start doing it more often, whether it's organizing a date night or complementing your eyes' "stunning" color.

2. Put the phone away

Okay, so this one could be a little cliché. You've been instructed to always put your phone away at the dinner table ever since you were a preteen; you've heard it enough from your mother, and you most certainly don't need to hear it again from me. If I know anything about smartphone addiction, which I do, it's how easy it is for that sneaky little iPhone to sneak in whether you're watching Netflix, driving in the vehicle, or, god forbid, having dinner with someone. As casual as a TikTok scroll may appear, cherish every second you spend with each other. When you're eating, talking, or enjoying a classic binge-watching session, put your phone away. Whenever you are together, be mindful.

3. Establish eye contact.

Intimacy happens in the small moments; romance need not be generated by great actions or in public shows of emotion. Eye contact with your partner actually has scientific support because it causes neuronal synchronization and the production of the feel-good hormone oxytocin. To put it in chemistry textbook terms, your brain feels more connected to another person through eye contact.

Focus on maintaining eye contact with your partner while you are speaking to let them know you are listening and to help them feel more connected to you (again, put the dang phone away!) But you should also look for smaller opportunities to make eye contact. For example, when you're at a party or in a crowded room, try to lock eyes across the room (there's a reason it's a classic rom-com meet-cute!) or maintain eye contact longer than usual in unexpected settings (but not for too long—10 seconds of eye contact and a cute little smirk is enough).

4. Incorporate a new experience.

Get out of your routines, whether you want to take a new cooking class or vacation to a different location. In addition to being enjoyable and exciting, trying something new will teach you something about your partner you didn't know and/or serve as a reminder of why you fell in love with them in the first place. You have been forewarned that you might actually fall in love with them once more.

5. Take a break.

Time apart can be beneficial, regardless of whether your usual relationship involves being joined at the hip all the time, like Mary Kate and Ashley were in the early 2000s, or whether you've been living far away for a long time. Spending some time apart will really offer your partner the room to miss you, and vice versa, whether it's only an hour at a hot yoga class or a weekend away on a girls' vacation. By doing your own thing, you can break out of your routine and have new conversations and things to catch up on. Self-care need not even be spoken about, but giving yourself permission to do what you want once in a while will boost your confidence. And everyone is aware of what happens when a woman leads with self-confidence... Spark!

6. Initiate a dialogue

When did you and your partner last engage in a meaningful conversation? A chat that didn't contain lists of things to do or occur right before bed? Talking about your future, showing concern for what the other person is thinking, daydreaming together, or reestablishing your needs in the relationship are all examples of sharing a genuine, emotional connection. Try to start a more meaningful discussion if your primary topics of conversation these days are "How was work?" or "Here's what we have to accomplish tomorrow."

Ask during dinner, "What is anything you want to do but are afraid to?" or, before going to bed, "What is your favorite part about our relationship?" According to psychology, it takes five positive encounters to every one bad experience (such as an argument or quarrel) for a person to feel that they are in a fulfilling, exciting relationship. Try to make the majority of talks interesting, humorous, or entertaining, even though it gets challenging. The rest can consist of ordinary tasks, arguments, or mundane scheduling.

7. Kiss

Perhaps when you were a teenager, do you recall that making out by the lockers was the thing to do? And because that was the only thing to do, why was it so absurdly thrilling? However, thank goodness, times have changed, make sure that your relationship still includes kissing. I don't mean general kissing; I mean spontaneous and heartfelt kissing, as if you were still in high school. Don't just use kissing as a technique to say hello and goodbye or to start an intimate relationship. When there is no expectation or any cause at all, give them a long, passionate kiss, whether you're going out to dinner, in the middle of a conversation, or just to remind them of your love at any time.

8. Give shared laughter a high priority.

While it's true that laughter is the best medicine, it's also the best-kept secret for preserving the spark. You know how you'll say things like, "Someday we'll laugh at this," when talking about a disagreement or an incident? Why hold off till someday? Nothing needs to be taken too seriously if you and your partner are in it for the long run; instead, try to find humor in any awkward situations or conflicts.

Watch anything that will bring out your sense of humor and help you develop internal jokes as much as you care about establishing trust. Bring up humorous memories, send your partner amusing memes, and flirt with each other as middle schoolers do. Nothing should be taken too seriously since life is too brief, especially when doing so dulls your spark.

9. Always try to impress one another

If you're in a long term relationship, your partner has probably witnessed your delivery of one or more children as well as your period's heavy days and post-Taco Bell bloat. Yes, your partner has probably witnessed you at your lowest point; after all, love is treating someone with respect even when they are at their worst. But can you still recall the times when you dressed up for them? Maybe you'd put on your best outfit for a casual dinner date or put on makeup for the first time simply to see a movie with your partner. Put out some effort to look and feel your best, whether it's applying body oil after a shower (it also serves as self-care!) or donning a pair of stilettos or freshly polished loafers for a dinner date. Harness the same drive to please them.

For this one, you two need to be on the same page. You're destined to feel underappreciated if you put out the effort and your partner doesn't care to notice or doesn't make an effort to impress you. They deserve a little more effort every now and again, whatever that effort means to you if they're the kind of person who makes sure to tell you how gorgeous you are even when you don't wear heels or contour flaw-lessly (who cares about that anyways, right?).

10. Take action rather than waiting for your partner to change.

If you are continually pleading with your partner for more romantic gestures or words, it may come across as nagging. Consider how much more you can give to your partner rather than constantly demanding things. If you're with the right person, they'll notice your additional effort and be motivated to put in more effort themselves. Give them plenty of love, and if you truly adore them, show it.

If all else fails, recall the actions you both took when your relationship first started. Consider how you handled them, how much you cared about their happiness, and how you treated them. Perhaps there won't ever be an end if you behave as though it's the beginning. Play the "Happily Ever After" song.

IMPROVING YOUR RELATIONSHIP BY BEING MORE SPONTANEOUS

It may become more difficult to maintain the spark as relationships develop and get older. And while it would be ideal for your relationship to feel exactly like it did in the beginning, the truth is that it could be challenging to experience the identical emotion once again. And it's not necessarily a bad thing; it can simply be a sign of how your love has evolved and solidified over time.

Many partners commonly experience what is referred to as a "dry phase" when it comes to romance. It's inevitable that there will be periods in life when romance seems to take a backseat, but that doesn't mean you can't be spontaneous in love at any time.

That is essentially the polar opposite of sticking to a schedule. Being unpredictable is necessary for spontaneity, which will heighten the tension and intensity in your relationship. Here is how to go about it.

1. Arrange a surprise vacation.

The easiest approach to bring pleasure and spontaneity back into your lives is to go on an unplanned vacation. Consider taking a weekend trip to a new location for the two of you. Together, you can have a redemptive experience while also rekindling some of the love feelings you had in the beginning.

That really doesn't require much thought or preparation. Choose a location, purchase your tickets, and depart the next day.

2. Staycation

Organize a haphazard staycation a little distance away, and enjoy each other's company. Staycations allow you to unwind and spend time with your loved ones while also being a less expensive alternative to traveling overseas.

3. Engage in unplanned sexual activity.

You develop the habit of adhering to everyday routines and following predetermined patterns over time, and this is probably also true when it comes to having sex in long term relationships. It's time to change some things up, regardless of where or how often you have sex. Just leave out any dull or standard motions that come up naturally.

If you know in advance exactly what will happen, having sex can become boring. The globe can serve as your bedroom if you make your sexual life more spontaneous. Choose a place and get going whenever the urge strikes if you have a little bravery and a partner who is similarly willing.

4. Try new things.

The next time you organize a date night, consider trying something new: a different restaurant, a different cuisine, or even making a delicious dinner together might reinvigorate your relationship.

It helps you both remember why you're together and that you still care about improving your relationship since it is so important to you. You could become disinterested if you start to think you know everything about your partner. Here, being spontaneous and trying new things can be really beneficial.

5. Attend a joint fitness class.

Let me rephrase the old adage: "Couples that exercise together and encourage one another to get fit together stay together!" Ask your partner to join you in a fitness class out of the blue—such as Zumba, yoga, pilates, spinning, etc. You not only get to be very healthy, but you also do it with your friends in a fun way. Also, having them there will keep you inspired.

6. Change daily habits

As you spend time together, unwritten norms regarding how specific tasks should be completed emerge. For instance, my husband is the one who checks the mail and takes out the garbage, while I am primarily in charge of doing the washing and dusting. Also, one of us always prepares meals while the other cleans up afterward on set days.

Changing these things up might be a terrific approach to bringing spontaneity to your life, even though doing something similar may be ideal for keeping things moving smoothly. Your partner will enjoy the surprise, value the kind deed, and possibly even respond with a fresh thought of their own.

7. Increase your listening.

Occasionally, paying a little more attention to and getting to know your partner will be the finest method to make your relationship more fascinating. Spend some time understanding what they are trying to say and what they need and want.

I recently expressed to my hubby that I was in the mood for something sweet during a casual quick phone call during work hours. He surprised me later that evening by bringing home my favorite dark chocolate and a slice of strawberry cake. These small details might help to keep the flame alive. Try to pay close attention the next time your partner is speaking, and come up with new ways to unexpectedly brighten their day.

8. Give a "Just Because" present.

Who doesn't adore presents? In particular, when you're at work and the delivery man comes to reception with a package, and you discover it's for you. Giving your partner unexpected gifts keeps the spontaneity and romance alive. You can send chocolate, a bouquet of flowers, or a bag of cookies with a sweet "just because" letter.

9. Discuss spontaneity.

Okay, so this might seem a little counterintuitive, but it's a great idea to discuss spontaneity with your partner. Tell them you adore them and how much you value having them in your life. To ensure that the spark doesn't go out, though, discuss working on some fresh concepts with them as well. Discuss ways to make things a little more haphazard, spontaneous, enjoyable, and joyous. Start making plans for activities and events that the two of you will love.

PLAN SURPRISES FOR YOUR PARTNER

Without surprises, a relationship can quickly become very stale. The last thing you want in a relationship is for it to become monotonous, predictable, or worse, stuck in a rut. You maintain the thrill and keep your partner interested in doing new things with you by planning surprises. Making an effort is crucial to maintain the strength of your love for one another.

You can easily fall into a rut when neither of you puts much effort forth after being together for a while. This lack of effort may manifest as not receiving birthday presents, failing to express your affection for your partner or even just being predictable and devoting all of your efforts to other pursuits. Even if every relationship is unique, and some individuals are rumored to dislike surprises, surprises are still vital and can be carried out in both little and significant ways. Remember, a surprise is when the other person is not expecting it; thus, it is crucial that you keep it secret.

Here are ten creative ways to surprise your loved ones in ways that will not only strengthen your bond as a couple but also inject a little humor into your relationship. Surprises usually liven up a relationship. You might utilize these creative ways to surprise your partner on your anniversary, their birthday, Valentine's Day, or just about any other day!

- Cook them their favorite meal
- Buy them something they've been wanting
- Make a homemade video for them
- Invite an old friend over
- Take them to their favorite place
- Hide notes for them to find
- Write them an old-fashioned love letter
- Cross something off their bucket list together
- Schedule a day filled with activities they'll enjoy,
- Serve them breakfast in bed.

STEPPING FORWARD AND PASSING ON THE INSPIRATION

WITH THE FIVE KEYS YOU NEED to build a loving, healthy relationship right here, it's time to pass on the encouragement and inspiration, and show other readers where they can find the same guidance.

By the simple gesture of leaving your honest opinion of this book on Amazon and/or Goodreads, you'll show other people where they can find the information they're looking for, ready to discover ideas and pass the inspiration forward.

Thank you for your help. Healthy relationships thrive when we pass on our learnings and experiences – and you're helping me to do just that.

CONCLUSION

I hope that this book has given you useful insights and doable actionable ideas for creating and sustaining a solid, satisfying relationship. The keys to a good and loving relationship emphasized in the book are mutual trust, effective communication, setting and upholding boundaries, handling conflict constructively, and relational self-care.

Each of these components is important to the formation and maintenance of a healthy relationship. We've solidified our understanding that mutual trust, which is crucial for fostering a feeling of safety and security in the relationship, is developed via honesty, dependability, and consistency. Good communication, on the other hand, entails active listening, empathy, and assertiveness and is essential for clearly and respectfully communicating needs, feelings, and goals.

Another crucial component that contributes to establishing a sense of autonomy and respect in the relationship is setting and upholding boundaries. Setting boundaries allows partners to express their needs, wants, and expectations while also respecting the individuality and different viewpoints of the other. Contrarily, the ability to manage conflicts and differences in a constructive and courteous manner through the use of active listening, empathy, and compromise is necessary for dealing with conflict positively.

We also stressed the value of relational self-care, which entails caring for one's physical, emotional, and mental needs as well as those of one's partner. Relational self-care promotes a sense of well-being in the relationship, which can improve the relationship's overall quality and durability. It also helps to build resilience, reduce stress, and prevent burnout.

One of the most significant things we can take away is that strong relationships require work, commitment, and active engagement from both partners and are not simply about love and romance. It takes time, patience, and commitment to create a strong, loving relationship, as well as continuous growth and learning.

The fact that healthy relationships are not perfect and that difficulties and disputes will inevitably arise is another important lesson we can take away. Healthy relationships can manage these difficulties positively, with respect, empathy, and a willingness to learn from them, which is what distinguishes them from dysfunctional ones.

Overall, the ideas discussed here, which are a combination of research, my personal experiences and firsthand accounts should apply to anyone, whether you're single and looking for love, or already in a relationship and seeking to improve it. With the practical, proven strategies provided and by embracing these essential components, you can take inspiration for your own roadmap to improve your relationship's quality, longevity, and general well-being, and also be able to enjoy the fulfillment and delight that come from being in a truly loving and healthy relationship.

FREE GIFT #2 FOR MY READERS

Just for you! Get this free ebook as my gift to you for being my valued reader. You will have access to 5 weeks' worth of journal prompts (a total of 35) which serve as your invitation to explore different aspects of your journey on the self-love path, encouraging deep self-reflection and nurturing a positive mindset.

Visit ebook.arianeturpin.com/selflovejournal or scan the above QR code.

ABOUT THE AUTHOR

Ariane S. Turpin writes about love, relationships, and family. Before she started her book-writing journey, she maintained a personal blog and wrote articles for her school paper in her younger days. Her personal experiences of love and heartbreak from her long-term relationships and pseudo-relationships, before marrying the love of her life in her 30s, as well as the wealth of learnings she has accumulated over the years are what inspired her to carry on this path. Her hope is that her books will help you be the best person you can be, and you can be with the best person for you.

She is an advocate for diversity and inclusion, and wants readers from various backgrounds to be able to relate to her books and find inspiration. When she's not writing, she loves to explore the outdoors and workout.

Visit Ariane's website to find out more about her upcoming books at www.arianeturpin.com .

facebook.com/arianeturpinauthor
twitter.com/arianeturpincom
instagram.com/arianeturpinauthor
tiktok.com/@arianeturpinauthor

ALSO BY ARIANE S. TURPIN

Unlock the incredible power of self-love while pursuing your goals. Take the first step towards an empowered life while you embrace your unique journey, celebrate your successes, and cultivate a deep sense of kindness and compassion towards yourself, even if you've struggled with self-doubt and setbacks in the past.

Available on Amazon in Kindle edition, Paperback, and Hardcover.

https://www.amazon.com/author/arianeturpin

REFERENCES

7 Tips for Handling Conflict in Your Relationship. (2020, November 13). One Love Foundation. https://www.joinonelove.org/learn/handling_conflict/

Alexander, M. (2020, September 23). *7 Keys to Effective Communication Skills in Relationships.* Seattle Christian Counseling. https://seattlechristian counseling.com/articles/7-keys-to-effective-communication-skills-in-relationships

Arikewuyo, A. O., Eluwole, K. K., & Özad, B. E. (2021). Influence of Lack of Trust on Romantic Relationship Problems: The Mediating Role of Partner Cell Phone Snooping. *Psychological Reports, 124*(1), 348–365. https://doi.org/10.1177/0033294119899902

Be Present in Your Relationship | Tony Robbins Firewalk Blog. (2018, September 4). Tony Robbins. https://tonyrobbinsfirewalk.com/be-present-in-your-relationship/

Bendix, A. (2019, April 25). *A relationship expert identified 5 warning signs of unhealthy love.* Business Insider. https://www.businessinsider.com/warn ing-signs-unhealthy-relationship-2019-4

BestVPN.com. (2019, February 13). *New Data Reveals Relationships Lack Trust as a Result of the Digital Age, BestVPN.com Reports.* https://www.prnewswire.com/news-releases/new-data-reveals-relationships-lack-trust-as-a-result-of-the-digital-age-bestvpncom-reports-300795098.html

Brigham, T. (2019, May 24). *How To Prioritize Yourself When You're In A Relationship | Life Goals Mag.* Life Goals Mag. https://lifegoalsmag.com/being-true-to-you-when-you-is-now-we/

Calkins, W. (2021, August 12). *How to Set Healthy Boundaries in Your Relationship.* Eugene Therapy. https://eugenetherapy.com/article/how-to-set-healthy-boundaries-in-your-relationship/

Conflict resolution - Healthy Relationships - love is respect. (2021, August 27). Love Is Respect. https://www.loveisrespect.org/resources/conflict-resolution/

E. (2018, June 27). *64 Percent of Americans Say They're Happy In Their Relationships.* https://www.prnewswire.com/news-releases/64-percent-of-americans-say-theyre-happy-in-their-relationships-300595502.html

Farris, M. (2022, July 18). *How to Manage Self-Care and Boundaries in*

Romantic Relationships — Counseling Recovery, Michelle Farris, LMFT. Counseling Recovery, Michelle Farris, LMFT. https://www.counselin grecovery.com/blog-san-jose/how-to-take-care-of-yourself-in-relationships

Feuerman, M., & Feuerman, M. (2021, February 10). *Managing vs. Resolving Conflict in Relationships: The Blueprints for Success.* The Gottman Institute. https://www.gottman.com/blog/managing-vs-resolving-conflict-rela tionships-blueprints-success/

Fisher, M. (2023, January 24). *10 Do's and Don'ts of Physical Intimacy in Marriage.* Marriage Advice - Expert Marriage Tips & Advice. https://www.marriage.com/advice/physical-intimacy/dos-and-donts-of-physi cal-intimacy-for-married-couples/

Gordon, S. (2022, August 22). *How to Use Words of Affirmation in Your Relationship.* Verywell Mind. https://www.verywellmind.com/words-of-affirmation-4783539

How to be Spontaneous in a Relationship. (n.d.). https://www.blueheart.io/post/spontaneous-relationship

Lmft, R. E. B. M. (2017, September 11). *Healthy Relationships Matter More Than We Think - PsychAlive.* PsychAlive. https://www.psychalive.org/healthy-relationships-matter/

Marie, S. (2022, April 18). *8 Ways to Build Vulnerability in Relationships.* Psych Central. https://psychcentral.com/relationships/trust-and-vulnerabil ity-in-relationships#what-does-it-look-like

MasterClass. (2022, April 18). *How to Build and Maintain Trust in a Relationship - 2023 - MasterClass.* https://www.masterclass.com/articles/trust-in-a-relationship

Mft, L. B. K., & Mft, L. B. K. (2018, July 20). *5 Tips to Practice Self Care in your Relationships | LoveAndLifeToolBox.* LoveAndLifeToolBox | Tools for Your Emotional Health and Relationships. https://loveandlifetoolbox.com/5-tips-to-practice-self-care-in-your-relationships/

Mindbodygreen. (2022, September 13). *What It Really Means To Have Words Of Affirmation As A Love Language.* Mindbodygreen. https://www.mind bodygreen.com/articles/how-to-use-words-of-affirmation

Pace, R. (2021a, February 1). *10 Effective Communication Skills in Relationships.* Marriage Advice - Expert Marriage Tips & Advice. https://www.marriage.com/advice/relationship/effective-relationship-communica tion-skills/#10_Make_communication_fun

Pace, R. (2021b, September 27). *10 Ways on How to Put Yourself First in a Relationship and Why.* Marriage Advice - Expert Marriage Tips & Advice. https://www.marriage.com/advice/relationship/how-to-put-yourself-first-in-a-relationship/

Pace, R. (2021c, October 18). *10 Signs of Feeling Suffocated in Relationship & How to Stop It*. Marriage Advice - Expert Marriage Tips & Advice. https://www.marriage.com/advice/relationship/signs-of-feeling-suffo cated-in-relationship/

Perry, C. (2022, May 20). *Say "I Love You" with 124 Love Quotes for Him*. The Knot. https://www.theknot.com/content/love-quotes-for-him

Raypole, C. (2019, December 13). *What Makes a Relationship Healthy?* Healthline. https://www.healthline.com/health/healthy-relationship#characteristics

Smith, M., MA. (2023, March 1). *Setting Healthy Boundaries in Relationships*. HelpGuide.org. https://www.helpguide.org/articles/relationships-communication/setting-healthy-boundaries-in-relationships.htm

Taylor & Francis Group. (n.d.). *Supporting Healthy Relationships in Low-Income, Violent Couples: Reducing Conflict and Strengthening Relationship Skills and Satisfaction*. Taylor & Francis. https://www.tandfonline.com/doi/full/10.1080/15332691.2011.562808

Tony, T. (2022, April 14). *How to keep the spark alive in your relationship | Tony Robbins*. tonyrobbins.com. https://www.tonyrobbins.com/love-relation ships/keeping-the-spark-alive/

What Does a Healthy Relationship Look Like? (n.d.). The State of New York. https://www.ny.gov/teen-dating-violence-awareness-and-prevention/what-does-healthy-relationship-look